ANSELM

OUTSTANDING CHRISTIAN THINKERS

Series Editor: Brian Davies OP, Professor of Philosophy at Fordham University, New York.

Cappadocians
Anthony Meredith SJ

Augustine
Mary T. Clark RSCJ

Catherine of Siena
Giuliana Cavallini OP

Kierkegaard
Julia Watkin

Lonergan
Frederick Rowe SJ

Reinhold Neibuhr
Kenneth Durkin

Venerable Bede
Benedicta Ward SLG

Apostolic Fathers
Simon Tugwell OP

Denys the Areopagite
Andrew Louth

Hans Urs von Balthasar
John O'Donnell SJ

Teresa of Avila
Archbishop Rowan Williams

Bultmann
David Fergusson

Karl Barth
John Webster

Aquinas
Brian Davies OP

Paul Tillich
John Heywood Thomas

Karl Rahner
William V. Dych SJ

Anselm
G. R. Evans

ANSELM

G. R. Evans

continuum
LONDON • NEW YORK

Continuum

The Tower Building, 11 York Road, London SE1 7NX
370 Lexington Avenue, New York, NY, 10017-6503

www.continuumbooks.com

First published 1989

Re-issued 2001

British library Cataloguing-in-Publication Data
A catalogue record for this book is available from The British Library

ISBN 0 8264 5773 8

Typeset by YHT Ltd, London
Printed and Bound in Great Britain by
Biddles Ltd, Guildford and King's Lynn

Contents

Editorial foreword

St Anselm of Canterbury (1033–1109) once described himself as someone with faith seeking understanding. In words addressed to God he says 'I long to understand in some degree thy truth, which my heart believes and loves. For I do not seek to understand that I may believe, but believe in order to understand.'

This is what Christians have always inevitably said, either explicitly or implicitly. Christianity rests on faith, but it also has content. It teaches and proclaims a distinctive and challenging view of reality. It naturally encourages reflection. It is something to think about; something about which one might even have second thoughts.

But what have the greatest Christian thinkers said? And is it worth saying? Does it engage with modern problems? Does it provide us with a vision to live by? Does it make sense? Can it be preached? Is it believable?

The Outstanding Christian Thinkers series is offered to readers with questions like these in mind. It aims to provide clear, authoritative and critical accounts of outstanding Christian writers from New Testament times to the present. It ranges across the full spectrum of Christian thought to include Catholic and Protestant thinkers, thinkers from East and West, thinkers ancient, mediaeval and modern.

The series draws on the best scholarship currently available, so it will interest all with a professional concern for the history of Christian ideas. But contributors also write for general readers who have little or no previous knowledge of the subjects to be dealt with. Its volumes should therefore prove helpful at a popular as well as an academic level. For the most part they are devoted to a single thinker, but occasionally the subject is a movement or school of thought.

Brian Davies OP

Preface

Anselm of Bec and Canterbury was excellent company. He told good stories, in fact such good stories that he became famous for them. He was perceptive and inventive and could, with the lightest of touches, make a commonplace event in an ordinary day memorable for the rest of one's life. Once he saw a small boy teasing a captive bird. 'That is how the Devil plays with us', he commented. But there was an uncompromising seriousness and austerity beneath his gentleness and his capacity to amuse. He was a man utterly given up to God, deeply and quietly intent on the contemplation of truths of faith which gave him spiritual, moral, intellectual and aesthetic pleasure all at once. To the disentangling of theological problems he would give endless patient effort and he expected those who lived with him to do the same, so that their understanding and their faith should be in harmony. His writings are not intended for cursory reading; they belong to an age when one read slowly and ruminatively, like a cow chewing the cud as contemporaries often said, in the tradition of *lectio divina*. They are intellectually challenging. But they are always clear and readable and accessible. Anselm went to a great deal of trouble to make them so, and his friends and pupils, even those of apparently most unpromising natural talents, found themselves spoken of as Anselm's 'philosophers'. He wins readers today much as he did when he was alive, by the attractiveness of a fundamental confidence in his faith, coupled with a willingness to discuss any knotty problem with an open reasonableness and evident enjoyment.

As a thinker Anselm stands high in any company. Within the

Christian tradition he rates among the best theologians of any age and the finest authors of spiritual writings. In an age when scholarly resources were limited and the tendency was to repeat familiar procedures and to reuse the contents of standard scrap-books of quotations from earlier authors, Anselm was a pioneer of a method of clear thinking whose tone can be straightforwardly described as a sweet reasonableness. His originality consisted not in challenging existing understanding of doctrine, but in finding new ways to reinforce and clarify truths of faith. Although he set out his arguments with the exactitude of a trained logician they never require formal training in the reader. And although he loved the unravelling of puzzles, not all of which seem as urgent or central today as they did to his contemporaries, he is never guilty of the trivialization of which Luther and others complained in the work of later mediaeval scholasticism. There is always an issue of perennial concern at the heart of any matter he considers.

His images often reflect the structures with which he was familiar in the society of his day. But it would be wrong to dismiss him as a 'mere feudalist'. Theologians in every age have had to contend with the question of the 'political' analogy between life in the world and the life of the Church. It was a major preoccupation of Luther and Melanchthon how far order in the Church ought to be understood in terms of monarchy, magistracy, or any other political conception. Anselm's feudal borrowings are relevant today, just as is Luther's understanding of German princely power, because they contain within the reflections on particularities of the political system with which they are concerned, elements common to the deep and enduring questions of order and structure in the visible and invisible community of the Church.

Anselm held in balance in his thinking an understanding both of the absolute justice and of the absolute mercy of God. The two are in part separated in his writings, the treatises being much preoccupied with the order of divine justice and its requirements, and the devotional writings with the gentleness and mercy of a God who comes to meet humanity in its suffering and striving. It is important to read the two side by side, and it is for that reason that the prayers and meditations have a place early on in this book. They are the setting for all that follows, because it is here that we meet Anselm most personally, and it is here that he lived his deepest life. On the foundations he laid in prayer he was able to erect the soaring structures of his reasoning.

Anselm's works

Anselmi Opera Omnia, ed. F. S. Schmitt (6 vols, Rome/Edinburgh, 1938–68); includes letters.

The treatises are translated in four volumes by J. Hopkins and H. Richardson (Toronto/New York/London, 1974).

The *Proslogion* is translated by M. Charlesworth (Oxford, 1965) with Latin on facing pages and the *Prayers and Meditations* by Benedicta Ward (Harmondsworth, 1973) together with the *Proslogion*. The *Cur Deus Homo* and the *De Conceptu Virginali* are translated by J. M. Colleran (New York, 1969).

See, too, *Basic Writings*, tr. S. N. Deane (Illinois, 1962).

Memorials of St Anselm, ed. R. W. Southern and F. S. Schmitt (London, 1969) contains the Philosophical Fragments.

Eadmer, *Historia Novorum*, ed. M. Rule (Rolls Series; London, 1884).

Vita Anselmi, ed. R. W. Southern (Oxford, 1962), with translation on facing pages with the Latin.

SELECT BIBLIOGRAPHY

H. Chadwick, *Augustine* (Oxford, 1986).

G. R. Evans, *Anselm and Talking about God* (Oxford, 1978).

D. P. Henry, *The Logic of St Anselm* (Oxford, 1967).

J. Hopkins, *A Companion to the Study of St Anselm* (Minneapolis, 1972); has a full bibliography.

R. W. Southern, *St Anselm and his Biographer* (Cambridge, 1963; 2nd edition forthcoming).

Abbreviations

C   *De Concordia*
Ca   *De Casu Diaboli*
Co   *De Conceptu Virginali*
CDH   *Cur Deus Homo*
G   *De Grammatico*
Historia N.   *Historia Novorum*
I   *De Incarnatione Verbi*
L   *De Libertate Arbitrii*

M   *Monologion*
P   *Proslogion*
PL   *Patrologia Latina*, ed. J.-P. Migne
Pr   *De Processione Spiritus Sancti*
S   *De Sacramentis*
V   *De Veritate*
VA   *Vita Anselmi*

References to Psalms give the Vulgate Psalm number first, followed by the Hebrew number: Psalm 33/34:10.

1

Anselm's life, Anselm's world

Eadmer, a monk of the Cathedral Church at Canterbury, wrote a biography of Anselm in rather the spirit of a Boswell, noting the sayings and actions of a great man as he observed them in daily contact with him. His purpose was profoundly different, however. In the late eleventh and early twelfth centuries it was usual for the monks of a house whose abbot appeared to them to be a man of exceptional holiness to seek to have him canonized after his death, and to look out for miracles even during his lifetime. Eadmer includes a long list of miracles at the end of his *Life*. He was setting out to do in an unusually personal way what a hired hagiographer would otherwise have been commissioned to do after Anselm's death; he had not known Anselm in his youth, or before he came to England, but he did his best to persuade him to tell him about earlier years so that his own gaps in knowledge would be filled in the most reliable possible way, by the subject of the biography himself.

There are other ways in which this *Life* is unusual for its time. Eadmer was no hired hack. He was a historian of note in his own right,[1] and a sane judge of evidence; he wrote more than commonly well; above all, he did not allow his conception of the shape the *Life* was to take to be dictated by the strict conventions of contemporary hagiography. It is a rare early example of a biography which will stand beside a modern one as a serious attempt to make a record of a whole man. But perhaps the most unusual thing about Eadmer's *Life* is the influence its subject himself had upon it. Anselm was not aware of what was going on. Eadmer says that one day at a stage when he had already copied onto parchment a good deal of his preliminary drafting on wax tablets, Anselm asked him to come and see him privately (VA I.lxxii, p. 150). Eadmer was unwilling to admit what he was doing. Seeing that he had something to hide, Anselm told him that he must either stop the work, or show it to him. Eadmer had had happy experiences of putting his writing under Anselm's eye and being greatly helped by his advice. So, in some relief, he showed him the work in hand. Anselm's first reaction was as he had expected. The scholar in him set to work, suggesting deletions and corrections, and a better order for the material, and, as was his way, he cheered Eadmer by his approval of certain passages. Eadmer felt some pride and satisfaction that his work had been thus 'fortified'. But a few days later, Anselm called him and instructed him to destroy everything he had done, because he thought himself unworthy to be celebrated in this way. Eadmer fought with his conscience, and at length he compromised by making a careful copy and then destroying the original as he had been told to do. We owe the *Vita Anselmi (The Life of Anselm)*, then, to an act of deceit within a friendship if not of equals, certainly of two serious authors. If there was vanity in Eadmer's desire to preserve what he had written there was also a sense of the importance of his subject and of the need to keep an account of an outstanding human life for the edification of posterity.

I

Anselm was born in 1033, in north Italy, at Aosta, in a mountainous region whose landscape was always to affect him. His parents, Gundulf and Ermenberga, were people of means and of good birth. His father, Eadmer tells us, was a generous, not to say spendthrift and worldly-minded man; his mother upright and virtuous, a careful housekeeper and an exemplary mother. Gundulf, shortly before he died, had a change of heart, turned from the world and became a monk (VA I.i, pp. 3–4). Anselm told Eadmer the story of a vision he had had as a child. He thought that heaven rested on the tops of the mountains he could see, and one night he was bidden to climb up there and go to the court of God, who was the great King of heaven. As he went, he saw the King's servants working at the foot of the mountain, supposedly reaping the corn, but doing it idly and as though they did not care. He felt indignant and decided that he must inform their Lord of what they were doing. When he came to the court on top of the mountain he found God alone there with his steward. He understood that all the household had been sent out to harvest because it was autumn. God asked him in a friendly way who he was, where he came from and why he had come. He answered as well as he could, and then the steward was told to bring him bread, with which he refreshed himself in the presence of God. When he found himself at home again the next day he told the story, believing, as a simple young boy, that he had been in heaven and been fed by the white bread of God. Eadmer does not comment on this story, either to say that the experience greatly influenced Anselm, or to identify it with the genre of visions commonplace in the hagiography of the day, in which a child's mother has a vision of future greatness before he is born, or the child himself is vouchsafed a vision like that of Samuel which indicates that he is chosen for the Lord's work. Its character suggests that it was a genuine dream and not a *topos* or stock story of the sort hagiographers sometimes put in for effect. It is allowed to set the scene for a childhood in which Anselm is portrayed as an honest, open and likeable small boy, who showed great promise at school—again a hagiographical commonplace, but in this case undoubtedly true.

The desire to become a monk made itself felt strongly in Anselm before he was fifteen (VA I.ii, p. 5). The local abbot would not take him without his father's consent. Anselm prayed for a bodily illness, so that he might be admitted on grounds of the danger of death: he had the illness he asked for, but still the abbot would not admit him. (God had other intentions for him, says Eadmer, people whom he wanted Anselm to help in forming in the future in another place, and so he did not allow him to be fixed there.) In due course this religious fervour cooled and Anselm began to be a rather wild adolescent. His love for his mother held him back until she died, and then, Eadmer relates, it was as though his heart had lost its anchor, and he was tossed at random on the waves of the world. God now stirred up in his father so strong a hostility to his son that Anselm was driven to renounce his patrimony, gather his possessions together and to set off across the Alps with a single servant. On the way he became weak with hunger and tried unsuccessfully to revive himself by eating snow. His servant, searching in their luggage, found there a piece of bread of miraculous whiteness and with this Anselm was refreshed for his journey (VA I.iv, p. 7).

For these stories, Eadmer must have been indebted principally if not entirely to Anselm himself. It is perhaps of some significance

3

that the next three years are passed over in a sentence (VA I.v, p. 8). Anselm spent them in Burgundy and in France, presumably in search of a master who could stretch his mind, for we next hear of him in Normandy, at Bec, where he went to study with the now famous Lanfranc. From this point Eadmer would have had access to more eyewitness evidence, for several of the monks of Bec had been brought to Canterbury by Lanfranc when he became Archbishop of Canterbury.

The school Lanfranc was running at Bec was unusual in that although it was a monastic school, it took external pupils. These, including 'the sons of the nobility',[2] provided a needed income for the new house. Anselm not only studied there, but became a valuable asset as a teacher (VA I.v, p. 8). He was by now possessed of a sound Italian grounding in the liberal arts and whatever higher education he had managed to get in the intervening three years; and Eadmer tells us that he was studying with great intensity under Lanfranc.

In this atmosphere his sense of vocation to the religious life began to revive and the need of a passionate nature for commitment reawakened in him. As he told the story to Eadmer, his motives were not at first edifying. He calculated that he was suffering at Bec all the inconveniences of the monastic life, its privations and hardships, without the expectation of reward which would be his if he became a monk. But when he began to turn his attention to pleasing God, he 'desired truly to become a monk' (VA I.v, p. 9). He then reasoned further. If he went to Cluny, then a great house of reformed Benedictine monasticism, he would not be able to take advantage of his progress in study, for there the observance of the Rule would leave him no time. If he stayed at Bec he would be overshadowed by Lanfranc. Eadmer says that he often used to tell this story 'playfully' in later years. He came to the conclusion that Bec was the right choice, for there he could truly be a monk in obscurity, because Lanfranc's presence would not allow him to shine. There were other options open to him. He was drawn to the idea of becoming a hermit. Or he might return to his family estate and live there as his father had done, but in holiness of life, ministering to the poor. Lanfranc went with him to see the archbishop of Rouen and together they persuaded him that the monastic life was to be preferred above all others (VA I.vi, p. 11). So at the age of twenty-seven, Anselm became a monk at Bec.

II

For three years he lived a life of exemplary devotion, while Lanfranc remained prior and Herluin, the founder of Bec, continued as its abbot. Then Lanfranc was appointed prior of the monastery at Caen, and Anselm replaced him as prior of Bec. In this time he read, and continued the read, the works of the Fathers, of which the growing library at Bec[3] had a good supply, particularly Augustine. His intellectual horizons expanded into the field of speculative theology. During the same period he became familiar with the Scriptures, both by reading and through the liturgy, in a way which was new to him. And his whole energies were concentrated with characteristic singlemindedness on the thought of God. Eadmer described experiences he can have heard only from Anselm himself, how he reflected constantly on the most puzzling and obscure questions about the being and nature of God and about the faith; how he formed the view that everything in Scripture was solid truth (*solida veritas*) and that his task was to seek to see into the heart of that truth by penetrating seeming obscurities (VA I.vii, p. 12). These preoccupations and assumptions pervade his treatises and it is clear that he was laying the foundations of future work at this time. His efforts were not merely intellectual. Eadmer gives an account of the spiritual exercises in which he engaged and his inexhaustible energy in teaching others what he was learning about the roots of the virtues and vices (VA I.viii, p. 14.). He fasted unsparingly, until he became emaciated; he stayed up long into the night giving counsel (VA I.viii, p. 14); he wept with desire for the life to come and for the misery of his own sinfulness. When some of those at Bec resented his preferment, because he was a comparative newcomer, and formed cliques and stirred up envy and strife, he behaved peaceably towards everyone and won his enemies over to love him (VA I.ix, p. 15). Eadmer tells many stories of his holiness of life and care for the formation of the young.

The only thorn in his flesh at this time was the burden of the administrative duties of the prior's office. (He was always to find such responsibilities distasteful and onerous and an unwelcome distraction from the serious business of life.) He went to the bishop of Rouen to ask to be relieved of his duties, but the bishop told him that he must not only continue but be prepared to accept higher office if it was entrusted to him. Anselm was already conspicuous, as Lanfranc had been, as a man of exceptional potential and a valuable asset to the Church in an age when able men were needed for a variety of posts (VA I.ix, p. 21).

For a decade Anselm wrote nothing for publication. Eadmer tells us something of the order and circumstances of composition of the early treatises, and Anselm's own prefaces and letters round out the picture. Eadmer mentions first the little group of treatises which Anselm himself says were intended as an introduction for beginners in the study of Holy Scripture (VA I.xix, p. 28; cf. Preface to *De Veritate*). These take as their subjects truth, freedom of choice and the fall of Satan. In a fourth, which he groups with them, Anselm wrote about technical issues of grammar and dialectic which have a bearing on the ways in which words in Scripture signify. The *De Grammatico* contains no theology, but much of use to theologians. Eadmer's absence from the discussions and teaching sessions which gave rise to these writings is apparent from his failure to try to capture the atmosphere of the schoolroom at Bec in Anselm's time. It may be that he had not even read this group of treatises as carefully as he might, for he singles out the *De Grammatico* as having the form of a disputation, when in fact all four take the same form (VA I.xix, p. 28).

We know from internal evidence that the *Monologion* was in fact Anselm's first book, and the prompter of the question of the definition of truth which led to the writing of at least three of the group of four intended as helps for those beginning on the study of Scripture.

III

During this time of contented monastic life as prior of Bec, Anselm was also writing letters, some on matters of business, and some to give advice to those who wrote to him (VA I.xx, p. 32). He regarded these as compositions of sufficient importance to have them collected[4] later and preserved. Eadmer quotes from a letter he wrote to Lanzo, then a monk of Cluny, probably about 1072−3. Anselm (who had a strong concept of the Devil as a person: cf. CDH I.22) describes for Lanzo the kinds of tricks the Devil will get up to to unseat him in the monastic life, making him discontented with his superiors or companions, or with the particular house in which he has made his profession. These dissatisfied thoughts will distract him from seeking singlemindedly the one true goal of perfection. If he notices that he is slipping into bad ways, he blames not himself but those with whom he lives. He must learn to banish all inconstancy and fickleness and to concentrate upon living a holy life where he is, bearing inconveniences patiently (VA I.xx, pp. 32 ff. and Letter 37).

Other letters of *amicitia* or monastic friendship to young monks now at Canterbury with Lanfranc are in the curiously elevated style thought appropriate for spiritual friendship.[5] To Gundulf, later bishop of Rochester, and to Henry, Anselm writes as soul to soul, employing exactly the same patterns of assonance and alliteration, antithesis and parallelism, climax and paradox we find in the prayers and meditations, and expressing a longing for the other's presence which is at odds with a gap of many years between letters. At the end of one letter to Henry, sent at the same time as another to Gundulf, Anselm instructs each to give his letter to the other when he has finished reading it, for what he has to say to the one is also for the other. We see here a contrast between the common-sense and entirely practical teaching of Anselm as spiritual director of the monks at Bec, his habit of enlivening his advice with little stories; and the sublime and aspiring height of spiritual friendship in which he tries to evoke the quality of the companionship of heaven as Augustine and he both envisaged it. Anselm was a gentle if firm master in the spiritual life. One abbot complained to him that the boys of his house were incorrigible and perverse. The more they were beaten the worse they became. Anselm exclaimed that he was rearing men to be nothing but brutes. If a tree is planted and then confined on every side so that it has no room to grow, will it not become twisted and knotted? If these boys are hedged in with fear and deformed by constant blows they will grow twisted inside with resentful thoughts. Of course they reject the teaching which could help them grow. They must be formed with encouragement and the gentlest and most carefully judged of blows if any are needed, as a goldsmith would form a leaf of gold into a beautiful figure. The soul inexperienced in the love of God needs kindness, compassion, loving forbearance, so that it may grow strong enough to bear tribulation patiently and love those who hate it. Thus Anselm won the abbot to see his fault by reasoning and by illustration (VA I.xxii, p. 37).

When, in 1078, Herluin the first abbot of Bec died, Anselm was his natural successor. He was deeply reluctant to take on the office and implored his brothers to find someone else (VA I.xxvi, p. 44). Only his recollection of the order of Archbishop Maurilius that he should accept higher office if it were enjoined on him induced him to give in (*ibid.*).

Eadmer's statement is borne out by Anselm's own consistent thinking on the question of accepting higher office, now and later.

Avoid office if you can, says Anselm. In an age when etiquette required those proposed for high episcopal positions to show a modest unwillingness, Anselm was genuinely without ambition, as he felt it necessary to protest in his own case (cf. Letters 156, 158, 159). He saw such advancement as a prospective distraction from the singleminded concentration upon God which seemed to him the true focus of life; and he found his fears realized. Unlike Gregory the Great and Bernard of Clairvaux, who saw and experienced the same danger of distraction, Anselm never made a wholehearted effort to balance the active and the contemplative life as a matter of duty; although he conscientiously did his best as archbishop it was with a sense of time wasted on business which ought to have been devoted directly to the love of God. He wrote to one abbot, probably William, abbot of St Stephen, Caen, who had asked his advice about the election of Hernost as bishop. It is Anselm's advice that anyone who can do so without breach of obedience (*servata obedientia*) ought to avoid taking on such a burden (Letter 52). To Hernost himself he wrote to commiserate with him over an illness and to comfort him with thoughts of heavenly reward if he endures his troubles in patience (Letter 53). Fulk, elected abbot, is advised that one should always take a humble view of what one can do and think oneself unworthy of high office, and never shoulder such burdens confidently. But one is caught between the sense of one's own weakness and one's duty of obedience to the will of God. It is therefore proper to try first to refuse, and only if the honour cannot be avoided without sin, to submit to it (Letter 61).

Where he is convinced that the candidate is unsuitable—and it was not uncommonly the case that someone well connected was offered a position when he was not really capable of filling it—Anselm is quite uncompromising. Lanfranc, nephew of Archbishop Lanfranc, received a fierce letter telling him not to consent to his appointment as abbot of S. Wandrille (Letter 137), and he proved so bad an abbot that Anselm felt it proper to write to the monks to say that he had been against his election and to commiserate with them over his cruelty (Letter 138). That said, Anselm respected office and holder as was proper by the rules of right order, to which he held in all things. A striking case is that of Gundulf, once monk of Bec and Anselm's intimate, who went with Lanfranc to Canterbury and later became bishop of Rochester. 'Once beloved brother, now sweetest father', writes Anselm to him on his election, changing the *te* of earlier letters to a respectful *vos*. He speaks of his 'elevation' (*exaltatio*) (Letter 78). To Gilbert, another monk of Bec, now abbot of

Westminster, he writes as to a fellow-abbot and 'father and teacher and pastor of souls' (Letter 106).

IV

Anselm never ceased to live as a monk and to regard himself as a monk under Benedict's Rule, from the time when he made his decision to stay at Bec. Again and again, he wrote to friends and acquaintances on the attractiveness of the monastic life. He wrote as abbot of Bec to advise the hermit Hugh how to encourage those who came to him for spiritual counsel. Two laymen had recently been sent by Hugh to Anselm, having come to him for instruction on the way to seek the kingdom of heaven. They had arrived with a request from Hugh that Anselm would send him a word of guidance on the way he should handle such cases. You will do it the more effectively, says Anselm, as you yourself hold on to the idea of the sweetness of heavenly life. It is nothing but a wholehearted adherence to God in love, together with all the holy angels and the faithful among men and women. The closer you come to this the more fully will your will be conformed to the will of God. That can only happen as you empty your heart of all other desire but the desire for God (Letter 112).

These remained the fundamental principles of monastic life for Anselm: striving with all one's heart to seek God; and the abandonment of self-will in loving obedience. The wholeheartedness extended to a missionary endeavour to bring others in. 'How long will you keep me waiting?' he asks Roger, who was delaying coming to Bec (Letter 76; cf. Letter 120, to Anselm's cousins). He holds out practical enticements to practical men. 'The divine reward will be of incomparably more benefit to you than any gift made in the world. Do not place your trust in worldly things, even when they seem to favour you, for they are being good to you only in order to suffocate you. What you see in the world's glory is not glory at all but a consuming fire. How much wiser you will be and how much happier if you leave the world and follow Christ' (Letter 81). In the world one's love is entrammelled and dragged down; remember the Lord's promise, 'Come to me you who labour and are burdened, and I will give you rest' (Matthew 11:28). The religious life offers that rest to the spirit (Letter 95). Of course it is not the case that only those who thus leave the world can be saved. That is quite true, Anselm admits to one Henry. But what is a surer or a higher way to heaven than to strive for nothing but the love of God? Those who remain in the

9

world are perpetually trying to couple one love with the other (cf. Letter 101). Certainly there are dangers in the monastic life too, but there are much greater dangers in the world (Letter 121; cf. 44, 46, 54, 101, 115).

There are letters to people with nascent vocations as adults. Letter 133, for example, is to an old friend of Ralph of Beauvais, of whom Anselm has heard good reports of his nobility of life. With a heart warmed towards him, what can Anselm do, he asks, but want the best for him? The best must be monastic life. Letter 134 is to Ermengard, whose husband wants to become a monk. Anselm has heard that she is resisting his wishes. What is holding you back, asks Anselm, from wanting the best for him and letting him go? Cases like these were becoming increasingly common. Anselm's contemporary, Guibert of Nogent (who writes of Anselm's visits to the monastery of Fly, where he himself benefited greatly from Anselm's advice on the spiritual life) is the author of an autobiography in which he describes the growing popularity of late entry to monastic life of military men who had served their time in war and run their estates and brought up their children.[6] Often husband and wife would enter religious life at the same time. This was a significant departure from the practice of centuries of giving children to monasteries as infants. It made the question of vocation all-important. And it raised entirely new questions about the teaching of novices (which we shall come to in a moment).

When Anselm won a soul, it was with rejoicing. He writes in holy delight to the novice Ralph (Letter 99). But his efforts did not stop at that point. His concern went on, to wake up those who might be growing sluggish in their love for God to new zeal and fervour (Letter 118, written to the monks of Bec while he was away in England; cf. 286, when he was away from his monks at Canterbury). His most substantial letter on the monastic life was written to the novice Lanzo, the letter from which Eadmer quotes (Letter 37). 'You have entered', he says, 'and been professed as a soldier of Christ.' You must not only repel the enemy with force, but learn his little tricks. Often he does not attack the new soldier outright, but more subtly. He cannot make him hate his new life, but he encourages him to be fussy and find fault with the place where he is in small ways. So he makes him discontented. Anselm was always anxious to discourage the widespread tendency to instability of this sort (cf. Letters 104, 113, 117, 119), because it was a breach of the obedience in love within a community which seemed to him one of the fundamentals of monastic life. If Lanzo can see that elsewhere he might find certain things of greater spiritual benefit to him than he has where he is, let him think either that he is mistaken, or that he is arrogant to imagine himself capable of better than his brother. If indeed his own house leaves something to be desired, let him submit humbly to the judgement of God in placing him there and he will not find himself held back in the spiritual life. Anxiety breeds negative consequences; taking delight in what one finds encourages the growth of love.

The spiritual life is a journey, in which one should be trying to make progress. Never relax your guard for an instant, Anselm advises the monks Herluin, Gundulph and Maurice. Each day ask yourself how you have advanced, and look to see whether (perish the thought) you may have slipped back. It is harder to recapture what you have let slip than to break new ground in holy living. Put the past firmly behind you and press onwards (Letter 51). This theme of journeying is to be found in Anselm's letters to lay people, too (for example in Letter 131 to the Countess Ida), but for monks and nuns he saw it as integral to their promise to live the religious life. Strive to make progress in the holy plan to which you have set yourselves, he advises Abbot William and the monks of Bec after he has become archbishop (Letter 178). He saw the community life as of the essence here, because of the mutual support in love which it provides. Take care of one another in love on the journey, he adds in the same letter.

Two letters exchanged between Anselm and Durandus, abbot of Chaise-Dieu, show Anselm's awareness of the monastic community as an ecclesial community (indeed it is usual to speak of a house of monks as an *ecclesia*). Durandus had written to ask that there might be a formal bond of unity (*unitas societatis*) between the congregation at Troarn and that at Bec. Anselm replies with a reciprocal request. The two communities are to pray for one another (Letters 70, 71).

The teaching of novices, once largely a matter of educating small children in Latin and liturgy and forming them in a life of holiness, now took on new dimensions with the arrival of adults, some young and eager to learn like many of Anselm's 'seeming philosophers' in the early days at Bec, but others older, experienced, and unlettered. Anselm thought formal academic training important. He wrote to the young monk Maurice who had gone with Lanfranc to Canterbury to urge him to keep up his reading (Letter 64). But we get a fuller picture of his idea of what was required in a letter to the monk Henry where he bewails his own lack of opportunity 'not only for writing, but also for reading and meditation and prayer' (Letter

50). The reading of authors—and especially of Scripture—ought never to be separated in Anselm's view from reflection and prayer. This is the 'Christian school' (*schola Christiana*) (Letter 49 and Prayer 15).

It seemed to Anselm important for a monk or nun not to neglect small things in the life of holiness. He writes to Matilda, abbess of Wilton, to encourage her to be careful to teach her nuns that one who lets himself slip into a small sin will gradually find others piling upon it, and that it is not only in outward behaviour that one must be constantly on one's guard but in one's thoughts. 'For you ought to judge it no less a thing to displease God by an unfitting thought than to do a wrong action before men' (Letter 185). The same warnings were sent to Eulalia, and the nuns of St Edward, Shaftesbury (Letter 183), and to Robert, Seit and Edit (Letter 230) and again, towards the end of his life, to Prior John and his monks (Letter 450). There must be no relaxation of vigilance even when times were hard. 'I hear', he says, praising the monks of Bec, 'that you keep rigorously to the order of your life even in poverty, with zeal to live rightly' (Letter 199). 'It is fitting for us to enter into the Kingdom of God by many tribulations' he comforts the prior and monks of St Albans, who have been showing a similar fortitude in their troubles (Letter 203).

But the dominant theme throughout his writings on the monastic life is that of obedience (cf. Letters 73, 182), which for Anselm contains within it stability and unity and all matters of order. The first principle here is that monastic vows take precedence over all other commitments. Even the *desire* to become a monk or nun[7] seems to Anselm to be binding in this way. He writes to the bishop of Paris, begging him to allow his chanter Waleramnus to become a monk (Letter 161), and urging that the Fathers held that the monastic life was the best way to live as a Christian and it is his pastoral duty as his bishop not to impede him in his vocation. He writes to Waleramnus to support him in resisting his bishop in the matter (Letter 162). Ermengard is encouraged to take the view that her husband's vocation ought to come before his marriage vows (Letter 134). Gunnild, who wants to give up her life as a nun and marry, is firmly discouraged from taking so retrograde a step (Letter 168). He tells her, gently, that it would displease the Lord. He asks her to compare the embraces of Christ with those of a husband, the purity of spiritual delight with the uncleanness of bodily pleasure. Here we glimpse the reasons why monastic vocation must take precedence over all other duties; it is a matter of choosing the better part. Thus, if anyone abandons such a life, as Gunnild proposes to do, and others among Anselm's correspondents actually did, he or she must be regarded as having been captured by Satan. Anselm writes in these terms to the bishop of Salisbury about the daughter of the King of Scotland whom the Devil has caused to put off her habit and live in the shameful garments of worldly life (Letter 177). The assertion of self-will is incompatible with true obedience. Anselm castigates the monk Hugh over a report he has received from his abbot that, although he is living as he should in many respects, he is fond of his own way and would rather do what he thinks fit than what obedience requires (Letter 232). A similar case at Chester, of a monk called Bernard, is reprehended too (Letter 233). Paradoxically, the will to be a monk, which should carry all before it, is in fact an abandonment of will to a higher authority.

The nature and identity of that higher authority occupies Anselm in several letters. 'Right order' is always the key. Monks who think it a higher calling to go on crusade are wrong, because it is their duty to preserve obedience to their abbot (Letter 195). It is essential to support the abbot of one's community and to obey him in a gentle and humble spirit (Letter 179). Under him, the prior and sub-prior are to be obeyed (Letter 182). But the bond of obedience works both ways. Anselm wrote to the monks of Bec when he was to be made archbishop and asked for their consent (Letter 148). To Ernulf, abbot of Troarn, he writes to say that just as he accepted the burden of his abbacy as an act of obedience, so he should not give it up except in obedience to the archbishop (Letter 425). In both the accepting and the giving up his own will in the matter has no place at all. That was his own experience, both in becoming abbot of Bec and in becoming archbishop of Canterbury.

Monastic profession, like baptism, is unrepeatable. When Ernulf was to be made abbot of Troarn, Anselm wrote to him to say that the principle of obedience to one's superiors under the Rule extends not only to the abbot, while one lives under an abbot, but to all one's superiors in the Church as long as one lives. So there can be no reason to renew or to take afresh any vow of obedience on becoming abbot (Letter 123).

As abbot, Anselm did as little formal business as he could. The administrative tasks of the monastery he delegated to others whom the trusted and spent his own time wholly in watching over the spiritual and intellectual growth of the monks. But where a serious problem arose, for example, over a lawsuit affecting Bec, he saw it as his clear duty to see that justice was done. In this we see already at work the principles which he followed later as archbishop of Canterbury (VA I.xxvi–xxvii, pp. 44 ff.).

In the year he became abbot of Bec, Anselm visited England. Eadmer gives two reasons for his visit. Bec had lands in England and it was important that the abbot should go to see them in person as soon as possible both for 'the common good of the brothers', as Eadmer puts it, and for the practical reason that an abbot was also a feudal lord, and it was necessary for him to take homage and oaths of fealty where they were due. But Anselm also wanted to see his old master Lanfranc, now archbishop of Canterbury, and to discuss with him one or two matters which were troubling him (VA I.xxix, p. 48). He was received with warmth by the community at Christchurch, Canterbury, and it is now that we begin to hear of his success as a speaker in the communities he visited (VA I.xxix, pp. 48ff.). He went not only to the lands of Bec, but to many other houses of monks, canons and nuns, and even to the great houses of noblemen. Everyone found him pleasant and approachable and adaptable (VA I.xxxi, pp. 54ff.). He taught everywhere he went, holding audiences rapt with his illustrations, which he was always able to fit to their experience and their needs. Whatever subject came up, he always had something to say by way of 'heavenly counsel'.[8] This highly successful visit to England was followed by others, as circumstances required.

The only serious cause of distress for Anselm at this time was the tale which was being told by one Roscelin of Compiègne, an up-and-coming and contentious scholar of whom we hear more in his conflicts with Peter Abelard.[9] Roscelin had picked up one of Anselm's analogies, in which he suggested that one might think of the Trinity as both three and one in something of the way it was customary to think of a single individual as 'literate', 'white', and so on. In Latin this device has a different weight from its force in English. 'Literate' can also mean 'a literate man'. The nearest English equivalent is to say 'Do you want the blue or the pink?' when asking someone to choose between two towels or shirts, and when it is clear to both speakers what the blue and the pink are. So in this way Anselm was seeking to express the paradox of the presence of distinct Persons in a single Godhead. But Roscelin claimed that he was saying that there were three Gods. This was Anselm's first encounter with academic in-fighting. He wrote a letter which he thought would clear up the misunderstanding, but he had not reckoned with Roscelin's temperament. Roscelin was not like the majority of Anselm's monks, simply puzzled and seeking enlightenment. Here was no reason prepared to be reasonable if shown the way to think. Roscelin answered back, redoubling his attack. Anselm was still debating how to deal with him when his life was turned upside down by the death of Lanfranc in 1089.

V

It was as obvious now that Anselm should be Lanfranc's successor as it had formerly been that he should succeed Herluin as abbot of Bec a decade earlier. Anselm was persuaded to go to England, at the entreaty of several of the English nobility, who regarded him as their spiritual physician (*medicus*), and who were distressed by the behaviour of William Rufus, who had now been king for four years. For a month or two Anselm occupied himself with business connected with the lands and houses of Bec. But the monks and laity of Canterbury had acclaimed him as archbishop on his arrival and the king had greeted him with joy, and it was not hard to see where the future lay (VA II.i, p. 63).

The circumstances in which Anselm was made archbishop caused him considerable anguish. The king became ill, and in fear of hell was persuaded that he must fill the vacant archbishopric whose revenues he had been enjoying for longer than the customary year. He chose Anselm. Anselm resisted the suggestion with every argument he could muster, and in the end he had to be invested with the episcopal staff by force at Gloucester where the king was in March 1093. There was a peculiar irony in this, for it was usual for a show of protest to be made as a token of modesty and to confirm that the new bishop had a proper sense of his own unworthiness for office. But there can be no question of the sincerity of Anselm's protests, and it was no small comfort to him in later years, when he discovered that he had inadvertently allowed a secular lord to intrude upon spiritual jurisdiction. The king presented him with the episcopal staff and it had to be held against Anselm's closed hand, for he refused to take it (VA I.ii, pp. 64 – 5, and *Historia N.*, p. 35).

The formal consecration at Canterbury took place in the presence of all the bishops of England in December, after a period of delay while Anselm brought himself to give his consent to his election, and a number of necessary formal stages were gone through: obtaining the consent of the duke of Normandy (Letter 153), the archbishop of Rouen (Letter 154) and the monks of Bec (Letter 155). He sent his abbot's staff back to Bec. He did homage to the king at Winchester so as to receive the temporalities of the See of Canterbury as their feudal lord. He was consecrated at Canterbury by the archbishop of York more than a month after his enthronement there in late September.

As archbishop of Canterbury Anselm inherited a pastoral charge of a different order from that which he had discharged at Bec. The English Church already had a long life as a national Church; like that of the Franks, and like the Hispano-Visigothic Church, in Carolingian times it had been governed by regular synods, under royal protection and at the same time as part of a single holy, catholic and apostolic Church which regarded the bishop of Rome as its head on earth.[10] We shall see something of the stresses to which the system was subjected by the Investiture Contest, and the rift between Anselm and the two successive English kings whom he served as archbishop. It was clear to him that spiritual duty came first, but it was never in dispute that he should also look after the temporalities of his see and supply soldiers and pay other such dues as feudal obligation required. Perhaps in part because of these unusual circumstances, Anselm's style of governance as archbishop was personal; he was not always able, for practical reasons, to work in collegial association with his fellow-bishops in England. Sometimes they sided with the king for their own advantage, and Anselm was left very much isolated. That he failed to call councils more often was not his own fault. 'I have asked', he says in Letter 176 of 1094, 'that a council might be called, which has not been done in England for many years, so that certain things might be corrected in that realm which seem intolerable.' In a similar attempt to put wrongs right, a council was held in London near the end of Anselm's life. The principle on which he acted, then, was that he shared as far as possible a common *pastoralis cura* with the other bishops of the realm.

He also took seriously the honour linked to order within the *ecclesia*. We find in English Laws of 725 the notion that 'whatever is consecrated, orders, and God's hallowed house, ought diligently to be honoured, for the fear of God'.[11] This orderliness of honour has to do not only with respect for those in holy orders, but also with a local and territorial responsibility which they hold, *mutatis mutandis*, in a feudal way. We see the first in legal enactments of 960 that priests ought not to be brought to trial before secular men, but that 'their equals be arbitrators and umpires', or else that they should lay their case before the bishop.[12] The second is underlined in Lanfranc's Winchester Constitutions, which stress that each bishop may preside in only one bishopric, and that he must respect the rights of a fellow-bishop to the services of his own clergy, not receiving any foreign clergyman without commendatory letters. Lanfranc also insisted that no one should ordain or receive a clergyman or monk who does not belong to him.[13]

Anselm had a strong doctrine of hierarchy in the Church, inseparably linked to his conception of obedience to superiors under God. A bishop may not ordain without his consent (Letter 175) as archbishop; he writes to Abbot Ralph about one of his monks who has been ordained by the bishop of Hereford, although Anselm had forbidden him. These 'orders' are never to be exercised by Anselm's permission (*nec illis ordinibus quos ab illo accepit nostra concessione aliquando utetur*); nor ought he to be reordained by another bishop (Letter 175; cf. Letter 200). Yet a bishop is supreme in his diocese. It is he whom an abbot consults when he wants to abandon his abbacy (Letter 186), he whose duty it is to protect the monks of Battle against the depredations of certain clergy of the diocese who are 'doing what they ought not' (Letter 172). The canons and the monks of a great Church serve God in their proper orders and the bishop must see that that ordering is respected by both (Letter 172).

Anselm was brought up sharply against the problem of the relationship of spiritual and secular authority in his relations with the two English kings to whom he was archbishop of Canterbury. It is not a matter to which he would perhaps otherwise have given much systematic thought. The broad principles of a ruler's treatment of the Church seemed to him clear and uncontroversial. A monarch should honour the Church as the Bride of Christ, he explains to Matilda, queen of England (Letter 243). To Humbert, count of Aosta, he writes along similar lines, grieving that the Church, whom God calls his Beloved and his Bride, should be trampled underfoot by wicked princes (Letter 262). It is the duty of those who have secular authority to guarantee the peace of the Church (Letter 288; cf. 284).

The problem at the root of the 'investiture' contest in which Anselm unwittingly became embroiled was the question of where the boundaries of jurisdiction lay. When Anselm writes a letter to Earl Robert and others who hold lands in the diocese of St David's to ask them to restore any of the Church's goods that they may have in their possession (Letter 270) he is addressing the matter at its most particular and local. But it had far larger ramifications. At about the same time, at the beginning of the twelfth century, he was writing to Henry I to protest because the king will not permit William, bishop-elect of Winchester, to receive episcopal consecration at Anselm's hands and has instructed him to leave the country because he insists that he must do so (Letter 265). The king regarded it as lying within his jurisdiction to decide the matter; Anselm cannot allow him to have rights in this question of spiritualities.

Trouble began almost at once when Anselm became archbishop. The king required money for an expedition to Normandy, and Anselm offered him the sum of £500 as his vassal. The King demanded £1,000 which Anselm refused because he thought it would place an unfair burden on his tenants. The king turned against him and Anselm left the court. What was already at stake was the question of first loyalty. Anselm always put his responsibilities to his own spiritual lord the pope and to his people before his duty to the king where the two seemed to be in conflict. Although relations were strained, Anselm was sent for to bless the expedition when the king was about to set sail for Normandy; there was a delay caused by a contrary wind. Anselm took the opportunity to address the king on the subject of various abuses he perceived in the running of the Church in England. William heard him sourly and declared that he would do nothing to please him (VA II.viii, pp. 68–9). Anselm began to feel the contrast between the peace of his former life and his present life of unwelcome duties and the unpleasantness of strife. He had been used to living in an atmosphere of loving co-operation, to seeing those he advised hasten to do what he suggested and to show the benefit of it. Only within the cloister at Canterbury could he live so now, and he found the community of monks there a haven from these new distresses (VA II.viii, p. 69).

VI

It was now to become his habit to withdraw when he had an opportunity and work in his study on some treatise. At present he was still engaged on the book which was emerging from his correspondence with the monk John over Roscelin's accusation.[14] None of his compositions went through as many revisions once published as this one did. It had been his practice not to allow his treatises to be copied until he was fully satisfied that they were finished. Partly because he did not at first realize that this academic controversy was a different exercise from anything he had engaged in before, and partly perhaps because of the disruption of his life during the period when he was made archbishop, this treatise *On the Incarnation of the Word (De*

Incarnatione Verbi) was to survive in at least two versions, and there is a good case for thinking that it went through more. The subject-matter was closely allied to that of his later book *On the Procession of the Holy Spirit (De Processione Spiritus Sancti)*. The task he set himself was to explain why only the Son was incarnate and not the Father and the Holy Spirit too; that is, to show in what ways the Persons were distinct from the Godhead. At the Council of Bari in 1098 Urban II was to remember this treatise, which Anselm had addressed to him, and call upon Anselm to resolve the related question whether the Holy Spirit proceeds from the Father and from the Son or only from the Father, in order to bring the Greeks back into unity with the West.

Nevertheless, despite times of scholarly pleasure and periods of refreshment among his monks at Canterbury, Anselm was under great strain in his years as archbishop. He wrote to Urban at one stage to ask to be relieved of his archbishopric because he did not see how to live without detriment to his soul (Letter 206). Eadmer describes how when there were disputes over matters of business or policy he would do everything he could to quiet them, or to remove himself from the scene, but if he was forced to be present he was greatly wearied in spirit and likely to become ill. The monks learned from experience how to help him. When such a situation arose, they would draw him aside and put to him some question about Holy Scripture. He would be distracted at once from his anxiety and as he plunged into the question and began to explain the answer to them his spirits would revive and he would return to normal (VA II.xiii, p. 80).

Anselm learned a good deal about worldly realities during these years. Some who had been his devoted friends before he became archbishop and could not do enough for him, now began to ask for presents of lands or horses. Those to whom he gave what they wanted were full of thanks and promises; those who were denied spoke ill of him and were heard to utter threats (VA II.xiv, p. 82). It was easy to see that he was gentle and simple-hearted and the ruthless took advantage (VA II.xiv, p. 82). If Eadmer seems to be painting an idealized picture here, it should be remembered that he was now writing as an eyewitness of life at Canterbury and that everything else we know about Anselm corroborates his account of Anselm as a man of God who stuck out like a sore thumb among the worldly.

It is not Eadmer's primary concern in the *Life of Anselm* to give an account of the political ramifications of the years as archbishop, but he does so in his parallel *History*. When the king returned from

Normandy Anselm went to see him and asked permission to go to Rome to receive his pallium as archbishop from the pope. The king responded angrily, saying that he did not recognize Urban as pope and that Anselm had no right to do so if his king preferred another candidate. This thrust Anselm into the now familiar quandary about prior or higher claims on his allegiance. As abbot of Bec he had recognized Urban II as pope. He could not now support a rival candidate on the orders of his king. He suggested that a general meeting of bishops, abbots and barons should be held to decide the matter, and he himself began to think that if the decision went against Urban he must leave the country (VA II.xvi, *Historia N.*, pp. 53–67). The meeting was held at Rockingham, and Anselm discovered that the loyalty of the bishops lay, for political reasons, with the king. Only Gundulf, bishop of Rochester and former monk of Bec, stood with him. Anselm argued that he must render to Caesar what was Caesar's and to God what was God's, making the necessary distinction between his spiritual and his temporal duty. The other side argued that he could not recognize Urban as pope in the king's realm without being guilty of treason. The bishops refused to obey any order Anselm might give them on Urban's behalf (VA II.xvi, pp. 85ff.) Anselm saw no alternative but to leave the kingdom. William Rufus swore that he would no longer recognize him as archbishop unless he renounced his allegiance to Urban.

It now became clear to the barons of England that Anselm's leaving was likely to have unfortunate results for themselves, and they persuaded the king to make a truce. The truce was not honoured. Baldwin, former monk of Bec and now head of Anselm's household at Canterbury, was driven into exile, as Anselm's chief confidant. But a compromise was patched together. Walter, bishop of Albano, brought the pallium for Anselm from Rome and the king was persuaded to recognize Urban and to make an appearance of reconciliation with Anselm (VA II.xvi, p. 87 and *Historia N.*, pp. 67ff.). Anselm wrote to the pope to thank him for the pallium and to apologize because he could not come to receive it in person (Letter 193). The uneasy settlement did not last. During a fresh expedition, this time to Wales, the king allowed himself to be convinced that Anselm had sent him sub-standard troops as his contribution to the army, and he became angry with Anselm again. Anselm decided that it would after all be necessary to go to Rome for advice about how he was to handle what were clearly going to be repeated difficulties with the king. William Rufus would not give him permission to go (VA II.xvii, p. 88).

When permission had been refused three times, Anselm decided to go without it (VA II.xx, p. 91). He left an angry king, but not without blessing him (VA II.xx, p. 93), and he called the monks of Canterbury together and warned them to expect trouble while he was not in England to protect them from the depredations of the king's wrath (VA II.xxi, p. 93). He says in a letter that all the forces of England (*vis Angliae*) cannot turn him from his obedience to the Apostolic see (Letter 261).

Anselm travelled simply, with Baldwin and with Eadmer himself. Where news of his coming preceded him he was met by enthusiastic crowds (VA II.xxvi, p. 102) and there was opportunity to talk to monks and laypeople. At Lyons Anselm paused, and sent messengers to Rome to ask the pope what he should do. He was unwell and he knew that he might not be able to complete the journey safely, because enemies of Urban II were covering a number of routes (VA II.xxvii, p. 103 and *Historia N.*, p. 94). Urban sent to tell him to come, and from now the party travelled incognito as far as possible. He was warmly received in Rome and Urban promised him his full support in his troubles. But while it was decided what was to be done, Anselm was to remain in Italy. It was summer, and hot, and Anselm was taken by John, a former monk of Bec, now abbot of a monastery at Telese, to stay in his own home village nearby, in the mountains (VA II.xxix, p. 106).

VII

It was here, in a period of relief from anxiety and withdrawal in scenery not unlike that of his boyhood, that Anselm completed a book he had begun perhaps as long ago as the winter he spent in England in 1092–93. During that winter he stayed with another of the former monks of Bec, now abbot of Westminster, and the only one of his monks to leave substantial writings of his own as a theologian. Gilbert was working on a *Dialogue* between a Christian and a Jew, and it seems likely that he and Anselm had conversations at this time about incarnation and redemption. Gilbert was concerned with the subject because it was here that the faith of the Jews most signally differed from that of Christians, and Anselm was working at that time on his *De Incarnatione Verbi*. When he had finished it, in the first year or two of his archbishopric, he seems to have given what study time he had to a new project, the *Cur Deus Homo*, a book of a quite different kind from the *Proslogion*, but which stands beside it as Anselm's finest work. It is characteristic that he should not have wished to be parted from the draft on his dangerous and uncertain journey to Italy, and that his first thought when he had the liberty was to get back to it. In his retreat, Eadmer tells us, Anselm lived in the way he had as a monk before he became abbot, following the Rule and spending his time in contemplation and in theological endeavour (VA II.xxx, p. 107).

In the summer of 1098, Roger duke of Apulia was laying siege to Capua. He asked Anselm to come and see him. The pope came too, and he and Anselm's company lived for a short time in tents near one another. Many were struck by the contrast; the pope's tent was splendid, and only the rich and powerful were admitted to his presence. Anselm received everyone in humility and simplicity, even the *pagani*, the Muslims of Roger's uncle's army, which had come over from Sicily to support the siege. Anselm gave them food and kind words, and they held him in profound respect; some would have taken instruction in order that they might become Christians, but for fear of the consequences to their safety in the army, and Anselm would not allow them to put themselves at risk (VA II.xxxiii. p. 112).

At this time Anselm was doing his best to persuade the pope to relieve him of his archbishopric, so that he could live in peace and freedom (VA II.xxxiv, p. 112), but the pope would not allow it. He asked him to wait until the council which was shortly to be held at Bari, where he wanted Anselm's help over the theological differences which had been separating Greek and Latin Christians since 1054 (VA II.xxxiv, pp. 112–3, *Historia N.*, pp. 105–6). Anselm, asked to resolve the dispute over the procession of the Holy Spirit, requested a few days' grace, and then gave the discourse on which his *De Processione Spiritus Sancti* is based.

The pope now kept Anselm with him in Rome, where he was accorded the greatest honour and always came second after the pope in processions, as Eadmer describes it (VA II.xxxv, pp. 113–14). Even the pope's enemies, some of whom made a plan to capture Anselm, were won over by the gentleness of his face and instead threw themselves down before him and asked him to give them a blessing (VA II.xxvii, p. 115). In 1099 a Vatican council was held in which Urban addressed himself to the Investiture Contest and pronounced with the Council a sentence of excommunication against laymen who 'gave' pastoral charge of churches to the clergy who were to serve in them, and those who received such 'investiture' from them. Anselm found these events disturbing. He perceived that he might be said, however innocently, to have consented to such an investiture himself when he was made archbishop (VA II.xxviii, pp. 115–16). When, after the council, he was given leave to go, he travelled as far as Lyons, where he was invited by the archbishop to stay, for it seemed unlikely that he could return to England while William Rufus was alive. While he was at Lyons, according to Eadmer, Anselm wrote two works intimately connected with the *Cur Deus Homo*. The first was the Meditation on Human Redemption (*Meditatio III*), the last of his devotional writings, in which he encapsulates in a few sentences the essence of the argument of the *Cur Deus Homo*; the second was a book *On the Virgin Birth and Original Sin (De Conceptu Virginali)*, in which he examines a complex of questions he had had to leave on one side in writing the *Cur Deus Homo* to avoid cluttering the argument (VA II.xliv, p. 122).

In July 1099 Urban II died and, a year later, William Rufus. To the surprise of onlookers, Anselm wept when he heard of the king's death (VA II.xlix, p. 126); he explained that he was distressed that the king should have died in a state of sin. The new king, Henry I, wrote to beg Anselm to return to England as speedily as possible (VA II.xlix, pp. 126–7). But Anselm felt it necessary to explain to the king as soon as he arrived what he now understood to be the proper procedure with regard to investitures. Although he had promised to show Anselm every deference, when the king heard this he was not disposed to defer to Anselm at all and for two and a half years there were bitter attacks on Anselm, because he would not submit to royal investiture as he had innocently done under William Rufus.

Anselm's natural instinct was to do the simple and direct thing. In 1101 he tried the plain tactics of telling the king what the pope wanted and the pope what the king wanted, and trying to bring the two together in reasonable discussion (Letters 218–19). Eadmer's *Life* becomes very brief from this point until he comes to the description of Anselm's death, perhaps because he was now continuing a work he knew Anselm had forbidden him to preserve; he could no longer honourably draw Anselm out about his thoughts and feelings; and he must have felt some awkwardness in writing at all. But the *Historia Novorum* gives a full account of the events of this protracted period of negotiation (*Historia N.*, pp. 120–47).

After Easter, 1103, there was agreement that Anselm should go to Rome in the company of a royal messenger, to discuss how the royal honour was to be safeguarded in the matter (VA II.l, pp. 127–8).

Anselm was warmly received by the new pope Paschal II, who supported Anselm's view and sent him back to England (VA II.li, p. 128). But Henry would not have him back unless he would submit to the king and deny his obedience to the pope. Anselm paused again at Lyons and settled down there in the house of the archbishop (VA II.lii, p. 130). The king responded by seizing the possessions of the archbishopric and negotiations proceeded uncomfortably for a year and a half (VA II.liv, p. 132).

There was a form of reconciliation as a result of Anselm's visit to France on his way back from Rome. He wanted to make moves towards improving ecclesiastical discipline in French territories. The king took the opportunity to make a sort of peace, and formally reinvested Anselm with the possessions of his see.

Meanwhile, Baldwin and the king's man William were sent to Rome, Baldwin taking with him a letter in which Anselm, in some despair, reminds the pope that he has gone into exile, leaving his see to suffer despoiling of its goods and apparently neglecting his duty towards it, only because he has had to put obedience to the pope and the cause of the freedom of the Church before all else (Letter 338). The mission was delayed by the king, and Anselm did not receive the pope's answer until April 1106 (VA II.lvi–lvii, pp. 134–5). While he waited he lived in Normandy, and only when matters were in some degree settled was Anselm sent for at Bec to come to England. He set out, but he was too ill to go on.

In due course the king came to Anselm at Bec and they cemented mutual goodwill by discussing the details of points on which they had been at odds over investitures (VA II.lvii, p. 134 and lix, p. 137). Henry was pleased enough to be at peace with his archbishop. He saw good hope of thereby subduing Normandy under his authority, and indeed he captured his brother Robert, duke of Normandy and succeeded in his aim, and everyone attributed his triumph to the 'merit' of his coming to an understanding with Anselm (VA II.lxii, pp. 138–9).

Anselm began work as archbishop in England again, but he was now becoming seriously ill. He was in his seventies, weak, and he needed to be carried about in a litter rather than riding upon a horse. But his mind was undiminished in its vigour. He was working on his *De Concordia*, a treatise in which he tried to solve the problem which had so much occupied Augustine and others after him, of the relation of human freedom of choice to divine foreknowledge, predestination and grace.

On Palm Sunday, 1107, some of his monks discussed with him the expectation that he would spend Easter in heaven. Anselm declared himself willing enough if that was God's will, but he said that he had hoped to live long enough to settle another Augustinian question, the origin of the soul. He was turning it over in his mind, and he said that he did not know of anyone who would be able to do the work if he did not (VA II. lxvi, p. 142). He grew steadily weaker, not in pain, he said, but unable to eat. On Tuesday evening he could no longer speak but those who were present asked for his absolution. He raised his right hand and made the sign of the Cross, and then bent his head where he sat. In the morning, while the community was singing lauds, one of those with him—perhaps Eadmer himself, for he studiously does not mention the name, although he says he was there—read him the Gospel for the day, Luke 22:28–30, which speaks of those who will be with Christ in his kingdom, eating and drinking at his table. Anselm's breathing grew slower as he heard these words, and those tending him moved him from his bed onto sackcloth and ashes, where he died in peaceful sleep as dawn was breaking (VA II.lxvi, p. 143).

Notes

1 Eadmer, *Historia N.*

2 Cf. VA, p. 8, note 2.

3 Two catalogues survive of the Library at Bec in the twelfth century. See G. Nortier, *Les bibliothèques médiévales des abbayes bénédictines de Normandie* (Paris, 1971).

4 See Letter 147.

5 Ailred of Rievaulx's *De Spiritali Amicitia* of the next generation is edited by A. Hoste, *Corpus Christianorum Continuatio Medievalis*, 1 (Turnhout, 1971).

6 Guibert of Nogent, *De Vita Sua*, ed. G. Bourgin (Paris, 1905).

7 On nuns see Letters 184, 185, 403.

8 Before he went to England, in Letter 80, Anselm advised the setting of an example as a means of communication where there was a language barrier.

9 J. Sikes, *Peter Abailard* (Cambridge, 1932), gives an account of the Roscelin affair.

10 See Y. Congar, *L'ecclésiologie du haut moyen âge* (Paris, 1968), pp. 131ff.

11 D. Wilkins, *Concilia Magnae Britanniae* (London, 1737), I.62.

12 J. Johnson, *The Laws and Canons of the Church of England* (2 vols, Oxford, 1851), I, p. 413.

13 Johnson II, pp. 8, 14.

14 VA, p. 72.

2

The man of prayer

We must set Anselm's theology in a context of prayer. He was the author of a series of prayers and meditations which were more popular during the Middle Ages than anything else he wrote and which attracted a multitude of imitators. They are the most personal of his writings (with the exception of some of his early letters) and in them we see the balance of intellect and spirituality in him in evidence as nowhere else. They are also the most triumphantly successful of his achievements as a writer. Anselm had a power of clear and graceful expression rare in any language, but particularly hard to hit in the Latin of the day without falling on one side into the fault of over-writing and elaborate word-play, and on the other into a crude banality. Word-play there certainly is in Anselm, but it is used with reserve and with a skill which matches figures of thought to figures of diction. A verbal climax carries a climax of ideas. An antithesis is marked by an assonance. A parallelism of content echoes a parallelism of sound:

> *Vaca aliquantulum Deo; et requiesce aliquantulum in eo.* (P I)
> 'Go apart to be with God for a time and rest for a while in him.'

> *Tendebam in Deum, et offendi in me ipsum.* (P I)
> 'I was stretching out towards God, and I was a stumbling-block to myself.'

In the treatises the clarity of the thought stands alone; in the prayers and meditations, and in those chapters of the *Proslogion* which wrap the chapters of argument in prayer, Anselm shows his feeling, and we glimpse the depth of the faith which was deeply interfused with understanding in him. 'I do not seek to understand so that I may believe, but I believe so that I may understand' (P I).

Anselm's prayers and meditations make something new of an ancient pattern. Meditative, private prayer had commonly taken passages from the Psalms as a starting-point. Anselm focuses his prayer by addressing it to God or to a saint—in itself a quite usual practice—but only as a starting-point for the unfolding of a sequence of thought at once devotional and theological. That is not to say that the saint is not important. On the contrary; Anselm evokes the saints he speaks to with such vividness that he seems to be in conversation with someone as physically present to him as one of his monks. Yet the conference with the saint invariably brings him to thoughts of God; never is the saint allowed to stand between the soul at prayer and its Creator, but only to lead to an observation or an insight. John the Baptist is Jesus' baptizer, and soon we are talking to Jesus.

These are unusual in any case in being private prayers at all. The strong tradition of preceding centuries was of liturgical and public prayer. But Anselm had in view a readership not only of monks but also of a leisured and increasingly educated laity; a number of women in the family of Gilbert Crispin, once a monk of Bec; and the higher-born Mathilda of Tuscany and others were known to Anselm and some were his correspondents. It may be that it was partly for this pious lay readership that Anselm began on his series of prayers to the Blessed Virgin. He says that he was asked to write a prayer about Mary by a friend whose name he does not give, and who may be no more than a literary device. The friend was not satisfied with his first prayer, so he wrote a second, and the still dissatisfied friend pressed him to write a third. Even this was a good deal revised after it had been copied and sent, so we may take it that Anselm himself became much involved in the writing of these Mary prayers and that they led him in directions he had not foreseen when he began. That is of some significance, for these were to be a major influence on the growth of devotion to the Virgin which was further fostered in the twelfth century by the writings of Bernard of Clairvaux.

These private prayers were to be used, Anselm insists, in an active and independent way by the reader. That is to say, they were not simply to be read, but taken as a starting-point for further reflections. One might begin anywhere. Anselm divided them into paragraphs so that they might more conveniently be dipped into.

What, then, is the theology to be found in the prayers and

meditations, and in the prayerful chapters of the *Proslogion*? It is here that Anselm first comprehensively treats the problem of sin in its implications for the soul, and draws out of it a theology of redemption and the sacraments. Topics which receive little attention in the treatises are here explored at length and with a painful wrestling and the repetitiousness of bewildered personal suffering which is entirely foreign to the calm bright air of the treatises. In the *Cur Deus Homo* we see the logic of redemption; here desperate human need and the immeasurable kindness of God.

Anselm is clear about the relationship in which the individual ought to stand to God. In the prayer to God he speaks of utter obedience, a life lived according to God's purpose and will. He knows that he falls far short of this perfect submission of will and action to God, and not least in failing to take seriously enough the fearful danger in which he stands. He seeks again and again to whip himself to a full consciousness of his sin, to experience the terror of conscience which some of the sixteenth-century reformers saw as the mark of a real turning to God. I am convicted, by the facts, of being a great enemy of God, says Anselm, but a horror prevents me from admitting it (Prayer to John the Evangelist, 1). 'How lukewarm is my soul!' he exclaims. 'My heart is hardened with stupor' (Prayer to Nicholas). The first of the three meditations is designed to stir up that recognition of sinfulness and concomitant fear of judgement which Anselm finds so reprehensibly lacking in himself.

We hear more about Anselm's conception of sin throughout the prayers. How evil and bitter it is! How easy to commit; how hard to give up! (John the Baptist). We are trapped and misled by our sins, he says, in the Augustinian tradition (*ibid.*). We are dead in our sins. 'I came as a sinner to be reconciled, and . . . I find that I am a dead man to be raised' (Paul). Anselm's overwhelming sense is of loss. He speaks of it at length in the second meditation. The memory of lost innocence makes worse for him the torment of present unhappiness. 'I am tormented by a bad conscience and its tortures in which I am afraid that I shall burn; I am tormented by a good conscience and the memory of the rewards of a good conscience which I know I have lost' (Meditation II). The impact of sin upon the soul is not its only penalty. 'The accused stands before the great Judge, accused of many great offences, convicted by the witness of his own conscience and by the Judge who has seen him sin with his own eyes' (Stephen). The fear of judgement is terrible, for the Judge is strict; he is angry; the offence against him is enormous (*ibid.*).

In the face of that judgement, Anselm seeks a forgiveness which will not only take away the fear of judgement, but also abolish all the consequences of sin in his own being. Forgiveness brings consolation, security, joy (Meditation II). Here Anselm explores both the forgiveness of the individual and the act of reconciliation by which Christ redeemed the world.

The prayers to Christ and to the Cross were written at the same time as the main collection, early in Anselm's career as a writer and about the same time as the *Monologion* and *Proslogion*. The third of his meditations, on Human Redemption, is much later and belongs to the period of the writing of the *Cur Deus Homo*. The prayer to Christ reflects the thought not only of Scripture and Augustine, but also of the Eucharistic liturgy.

The whole is a lifting up of the soul in thanksgiving for redemption. Anselm sees his soul as trying to 'pay its debt' by praise and thanks, as able to make such an effort for good only because Christ has made it possible ('If my soul wills any good, you gave it to me'). By remembering Christ's work he is set on fire with love. Yet when he tries to bring the Passion before him as a historical scene he has a desperate sense of failure because he was not there. He treats the reader to a dramatic reconstruction of the most intense vividness: 'Why were you not there, my soul, to be pierced by a sword of bitter sorrow when you could not bear to see your Saviour pierced with a lance?. . . Why did you not feel horror to see the blood that poured out of your Redeemer's side?. . . Why did you not share the sufferings of his mother?' He speaks to the Virgin: 'My most merciful Lady, what am I to say about the tears which sprang from your most pure eyes when you saw your only Son before your eyes, bound, beaten and wounded?' He imagines himself with Joseph: 'O that I might have taken my Lord down from the Cross with fortunate Joseph and . . . laid him in the tomb, or even followed after'. Now Anselm feels bereft. All this it was denied him to see. He was not there. His Lord has ascended and like the Bride of the Song of Songs his soul is left longing. 'Where shall I go? Where shall I seek him? Where and when shall I find him?' Anselm prays for the comfort of his Lord's presence. In a single sequence Anselm compresses a whole soteriology. The soul is enabled to turn to Christ and to begin to want the good, but with gladness and thanksgiving goes an awakened longing which is unsatisfied this side of heaven and which leads the soul on endlessly in search of a Lord already possessed. Anselm expresses the paradox in this way: 'Give me what you have made me want'.

The prayer to the Cross has a place in a tradition of veneration of the Cross which is very ancient and had an established liturgical place in Anselm's day. Anselm uses the Cross as a starting-point for contemplation of that which the image of the Cross before him represents, the true Cross, 'and by that Cross', he says, 'I adore our merciful Lord, and what he has done in mercy for us'. He rehearses what the Cross has done as God's instrument in Christ's work. His emphasis throughout is upon Christ's willingness. 'He chose you, that he might do what he would in his goodness'—save sinners from death, destroy death itself, save the condemned, bring life to the dead, despoil hell, renew the world and make it beautiful with truth, restore the heavenly city and perfect it. He sees the Cross as itself 'exalted' by that work which was accomplished upon it, so that he can say, 'in you and through you is my life and salvation . . . and all my good'. It remains for him a powerful instrument for good: 'I am sure that if I give thanks, love and live to your glory, I shall at last come to . . . eternity . . . through you'. Here, as in the prayer to Christ, we see a full theology of the world's redemption coupled with an intimate sensitivity to the working out of salvation in the individual soul, a sense of the vastness and completeness of what was brought about once and for all by Christ's death, and of the inadequacy and uncertainty of a human response which needs that work applied again and again throughout life if the soul is to 'come to those good things for which man was created' (Prayer to the Cross).

II

The Meditation on Human Redemption brings us to an older and more sober Anselm, in whom there is less of the ebullient word-play and daring ideas of the early devotional works. Here he unfolds a *Cur Deus Homo* in miniature. He asks in prayer why Christ hid his power in the humility of the incarnation and the death of the Cross. He holds up the great paradox: 'You did not assume human nature to hide what was known about you, but to reveal what was unknown'. He dispatches, as he does in the *Cur Deus Homo*, the notion that the Devil had any rights in the matter, that Christ's death was in any sense a payment of ransom to Satan. It was not this necessity which 'made the highest so humble himself', but a necessity which is more accurately called need. Human nature needed to make amends to God in this way, says Anselm; God had no need to suffer so; but for the sake of man, and because man could not do it for himself, Christ humbled himself in mercy to do what was necessary. Man could not be restored to the state in which he was created unless he could be purified of sin and become sinless like the angels. That could come about only if he received forgiveness for all his sins, and only if he made full satisfaction was that possible. Satisfaction required that the sinner gave to God something which he did not owe him, something of greater value than everything which is not God himself. It was not merely a matter of making up for the sin itself but of restoring God's honour by going beyond and honouring him with a gift. But only from God himself could such a gift come. God himself, in the person of Christ, took on himself all the debt which sinners owed, when he himself owed nothing, and freely and willingly made reparation to God for man, as himself fully a man. And in this divine nature was not humbled, though on the face of it, it must seem so. Instead, human nature was unimaginably exalted.

Anselm sets out the steps of the argument here without the full details he gives in the *Cur Deus Homo*, but so that its force is plain. He makes it a prelude to an account of his own experience of redemption. Christ was in darkness, descending into hell, a huge lead weight round his neck dragging him down, unbearably burdened. So it was with Anselm: 'Thus was I placed'. Then like the sun, Christ gave him light. The weight under which Anselm lay and which was inexorably dragging him down to hell was the burden of original sin which he had from his first parents. He faced demon enemies, doing their best to make him commit a multitude of actual sins, for which also he was to be damned. Christ removed the original sin and the condemnation which went with it. He made Anselm his own and acknowledged him. He set him upright and lifted his head to know and love him. He made him sure that his soul would be saved, 'For you have given your life for it, and you have promised me your glory if I follow you', says Anselm.

Yet all is not well with him. 'I owe you more than my whole self', he says, but he cannot find that 'more' to give; he cannot even give his whole self. He is conscious of a lifetime's need of help if he is to realize and enter into the good Christ has given him.

It is here that we move into the area of the theology of the Church, ministry and sacrament of which Anselm says relatively little in his treatises. There are perhaps two reasons for that. His natural bent, as we shall see, was for those aspects of theology which are closest to philosophy, for the pure air of the contemplation of God in himself. It was to these topics that he devoted his first treatises, the *Monologion* and *Proslogion*. Under the pressure of contemporary controversy he explored questions concerning incarnation and redemption and the 'most famous question' of the relationship between human free choice and divine grace, predestination and foreknowledge, and he discovered there scope for an investigation which satisfied him both intellectually and spiritually (for we see traces of his reflections in the prayers and meditations). But his mind was not naturally drawn to matters of ecclesiology, ministry and sacrament by any need to understand them better; nor was he forced to explore their ramifications by the challenge of current controversy, although, as we shall see, his letters reveal a characteristically clear and comprehensive grasp. (The sole exception here might have been the theology of the Eucharist, but the debate on transubstantiation between his former master Lanfranc and the grammarian Berengar was one from which he seems deliberately to have kept himself apart.) But the lack of any comprehensive treatment of these subjects in the treatises most certainly does not mean that they were not important to Anselm. The material in the prayers and meditations gives us a glimpse of his views on topics which became, in the later Middle Ages and in the sixteenth century, of incalculable importance for the future of Western Christendom, and, slight though the indications are, they enable us to round out the picture of Anselm's theology which is to be had from the treatises and see his Christianity in the round.

III

We can best begin with the prayer to Mary Magdalene. Mary, says Anselm, knows by her own life 'how a sinful soul can be reconciled with its creator', 'what counsel a soul in misery needs', 'what medicine' will restore a sick soul to health. Anselm holds a broadly Augustinian view of predestination. Mary is one of the 'chosen'. But he couples it with the picture of a loving friendship between the soul and its Redeemer which pervades the prayers and meditations and with which the theme of longing and inadequacy in all the prayers is shot through as with gold. You are, he says to Mary, 'now with the chosen because you are beloved'; 'you are beloved because you are chosen of God'. The divine Gardener planted her soul in his garden. What he plants he also waters, but that watering is also a testing. Like the Bride of the Song of Songs, she burns with anxiety, seeking him, desiring him, asking for him. 'For love's sake he cannot bear her grief for long'; he does not go on hiding himself. 'For the sweetness of love he shows himself.' She responds to the sound of the gentle voice in which he has been accustomed to call her by name. She is transformed, her sorrow gone and replaced by joy. This is the pattern of the soul's reconciliation, her discovery of friendship with her Lord who chooses her and makes her his own.

Anselm understands forgiveness as embracing not only himself but the whole Christian community, his enemies as well as his friends. 'I ask this punishment for those who serve with me and hate me', he says, 'Let us love you and each other . . . so that we may make amends . . . for our own offences and for one another's offences', and 'so that we may obey one Lord and one Master with one heart in love' (Prayer for Enemies). He knows that he is not succeeding as he would wish in forgiving those who are his enemies, 'but my will is set to do it', he promises (*ibid.*). For his friends he prays diffidently, as one not worthy to ask forgiveness even for himself, but as united with them in the community of love, with the Source of love, 'by whose command and gift' he loves them.

It is as standing within this community of love and friendship and mutual help that he prays to the saints as his helpers. To John the Evangelist he says that one who because of his sins feels the need of someone to intercede for him, turns naturally to the saint who is well known for his friendship with the Judge whom Anselm has cause to fear. 'What power you have through that same friendship!', he cries. To Nicholas, Benedict, Stephen, he speaks as an unworthy friend in need of someone to ask on his behalf for that which he dare not ask. They stand secure in their friendship with Christ. They have merit in his eyes, where Anselm has none, and he begs them to plead their deserving on his behalf.

Embedded here is a doctrine of ministry, which, like much of what Anselm has to say about the Church's role in the working out of salvation and the penitential system, appears embryonic in comparison with the maturing treatment of these matters in succeeding centuries. But it is a doctrine clear and strong in its main lines, so that it is apparent where Anselm would have stood in the discussions of later periods. Anselm sees ministry in the Church as primarily a matter of pastoral care, as Gregory the Great had done. The Prayer to St Peter addresses Peter as shepherd of the flock of God. It also calls him 'Prince', able to bind and loose at will, to heal and raise up, to give the kingdom of heaven to whom he will. But Anselm does not see him as the proud ecclesiastical potentate of the later mediaeval debates. 'I need your help', he says, and he sets the need for Peter's power side by side with the need for his kindness. If

Anselm is sunk so low in his trouble that his cry cannot be heard by Peter, he begs him to bend down in goodness to listen. 'Have a care, kind shepherd, for the lamb of the flock which has been entrusted to you.' Anselm is a sickly sheep, lying at the shepherd's feet. But both stand before the Lord of the shepherd and the sheep. The sheep shows his shepherd his injuries, which he incurred when he strayed, the sore places he has had for a long time and which have been neglected. If the shepherd is inclined to ignore him, Anselm reminds him that he too is a sheep who has gone astray, denied his Lord three times, and himself stood in need of love and mercy. Peter's is a high office, but his office is to have mercy, to imitate his Lord as an apostle, as door-keeper of heaven to show a mercy which admits the unworthy sinner even though he has not known all his sins to confess them and has not sufficiently made amends and done penance as he should. Peter's ministry is empowered by the mercy shown to him, and he and his sheep stand side by side before their Lord as equals in the community of love made possible by divine mercy.

Anselm can be seen in many passages in the prayers to be taking it for granted that works have merit, and that there is a place for a formal process of confession, satisfaction and absolution. The complete forgiveness of baptism with its grace (though not its eternal benefits) is lost by the sinner and needs to be renewed. 'Give me back through the sorrow of penitence what you gave before in the sacrament of baptism', he pleads (Prayer to John the Baptist). In the prayer to be said by the consecrating priest before receiving the Body and Blood of Christ, he makes it plain that he understands the Eucharist to be efficacious. In the consecrated elements he adores the Lord and thanks him for the gift of his Body and Blood. He desires to receive it, 'as cleansing from sin' and as 'a defence against sin'. He knows his own unworthiness, but he 'presumes' to receive these gifts so that he may be 'justified' by them. They will be for his forgiveness and protection.

These points are wholly uncontroversial for Anselm. He receives them in simplicity. Nowhere does he query the compatibility of a doctrine of election with the notion that we must work for our salvation; of his security in faith with his anxiety to do well for his Lord; of his joy and thankgiving with his sense of oppression and desolation because of sin. These are the attitudes of a mind and heart fundamentally unanxious about the facts of faith and experienced in the vicissitudes of growth in holiness. Anselm, like others in the mediaeval world, was conscious in his daily life of the complexities of living out the process of sanctification, and of its interpenetration with the absoluteness of justification to which sixteenth-century reformers pointed.

We shall hear more of these matters in the chapters which follow. But they have a place in this preliminary sketch, because the prayers and meditations make it plain that they were the stuff of his spiritual life, and his daily and most intense preoccupation as a monk and *a fortiori* as a Christian. As we go on to more speculative stuff, we shall do well to bear in mind the picture the devotional writings give us of the whole Anselm.

3

Doing theology

In the prayers and meditations we see an Anselm constantly reaching out towards a God from whom he feels himself separated by sin. He speaks of his lukewarmness, the inadequacy of his response, the feebleness of his desire. All this is conventional enough in spiritual writing. But here it is coupled with a deep sense of security and Anselm is discovered again and again in conversation with a friend. Where the friend is a saint, it is, as Ailred of Rievaulx was to put it in his treatise on spiritual friendship in the generation after Anselm, as though the conversation were three-cornered. With the friends who are talking, Christ is present, making a third.

This duality of the sense of being very far below a God who is unimaginably remote from human understanding, and the knowledge of a God who is a friend, pervades Anselm's treatises. In his first book, the *Monologion*, he suggests that the way to get an idea of a God who is the highest good is to climb up a ladder of goods in one's mind, beginning with the familiar good things of everyday life. A profoundly Platonic conception of the Supreme Being is thus as it were tethered to common experience and a God ultimately unknowable by human intellect is presented in human terms.

Behind all this lies the furnishing of Anselm's mind over many years, first with the training in grammar, logic and rhetoric which he would have had as a youth in Italy; then with higher studies, especially in logic, got during his time in Burgundy and France travelling from master to master and finally settling at Bec under Lanfranc; then, when he became a monk, with ten years of reading of Scripture and the Fathers, especially Augustine, before he began to write.

The writing itself was the product of teaching. We know that he did some teaching in the school at Bec while Lanfranc was there. He wrote to one young monk, Maurice, whom Lanfranc took with him when he left Bec, to encourage him to go on systematically with his reading (Letter 64). An ambitious father wrote to him to enquire whether he would take on his son as a pupil (Letters 19−20). But Anselm found the parsing and patient reading of Latin authors tedious (*molestum* is his word), and when Lanfranc left Bec and the character of the school changed, Anselm did not attempt to maintain its reputation in the world at large as a place where external pupils, the sons of local nobility (and many from further afield), could get an educational start in life.

He began to teach in a quite different style. The account which Orderic Vitalis later wrote in his history of the period describes all the monks of Bec as 'seeming philosophers'. Anselm was teaching them to think. He did so within a wholly monastic tradition of meditation. The *Monologion* itself is called a *meditatio*. But the quiet roaming of the devout mind as it grazes a patch of Scripture or one of the Fathers, the 'chewing' and 'sucking' of which Anselm himself speaks approvingly in the context of prayer, are overlaid and informed by a rigorous intellectual discipline. Although, as Anselm pointed out to Lanfranc in some indignation when he questioned whether the *Monologion* was properly founded upon Scripture and the Fathers, he was careful to ensure that his words were in keeping with the authorities, he does not allow the texts to shape the overall sequence of the thought.

It is hard to emphasize sufficiently how unusual this was. All of Anselm's contemporaries, and his predecessors for many generations, had proceeded by commenting on a text or by quoting a series of passages and perhaps linking them loosely together. Anselm wrote no commentaries, and the thorough Augustinianism of his earliest work makes itself apparent not in quotations but in the deep structure of the thought and in the assumptions on which he works. Even Scripture is characteristically employed in worked examples, designed to teach the user the way to approach other tasks of textual criticism, to equip him with a method, rather than to illustrate and support an argument.

We can get a glimpse of the atmosphere of Anselm's colloquies with his young monks in the opening passages of the treatise he wrote *On Truth* after he had finished the *Monologion*. He chose, as he commonly did, a dialogue form which he would have seen Augustine using to good effect in many of his own treatises. The pupil puts a question. We believe that God is truth. But we also say that there is truth in many other things. Does this mean that truth in all the forms it takes is itself God? He reminds Anselm of one of his arguments in the *Monologion* and points out that, although he had shown there that the Supreme Truth has no beginning and no end, he had not arrived at a definition of truth. In this (presumably) fictional device by which Anselm introduces a topic over which he himself clearly had a sense of unfinished business, we hear the echo of real queries put by pupils whose minds were being philosophically trained.

Anselm suggests that they should look into the definition of truth together. He employs broadly the same method as that first sketched at the beginning of the *Monologion*, examining examples of what is to be described or defined so as to discover what they have in common. He begins by asking the pupil to try to say when a proposition is true. The pupil suggests that one can say a proposition is true when what is says exists really does exist and when what it denies to exist really does not exist. Is the thing so affirmed or denied the truth of the proposition, then? asks Anselm. No, concedes the pupil. The truth lies in the thing, but it is not itself the thing. The thing affirmed or denied is somehow the cause of the proposition's being true; it looks as though the truth is 'in' the proposition. Anselm encourages him to probe further. Where in the proposition would this truth be? Would it be in its signification, or its definition, or could it be that the proposition is itself the truth?

The pupil realizes that the same proposition can sometimes be true and sometimes false (for example if I say, 'I am now in Rome'), and that if the truth were in its signification or its definition, it would always be true. Its truth must lie somewhere in the relationship between the proposition and that to which it refers as being or not being the case. Anselm presses his pupil further. He makes him distinguish between 'correctness' (signifying what the proposition should) and 'truth' (signifying that what is so is so). A proposition may be said to have received a power of signifying, and so long as it does that as it ought it is signifying correctly. The proposition 'It is day' is designed to signify that it is day, and so long as it does that it does its job. It can do so independently of whether it is in fact day (V 2).

The pupil is led, gradually, to perceive that truth consists in rightness. This notion proves to hold for truth in thoughts, truth of will and actions and sense, and so we go on to learn that the truth in all things is one and the same truth. The dialogue is in some measure Socratic (although Anselm would not have known Plato's dialogues),[1] but the master's method is gentler. The pupil is challenged and encouraged to think for himself and put right when he is on the wrong track, but he is not made a fool of. In the gentle enquiries of Anselm's schoolroom his pupils would have found that they could indeed 'do philosophy', and also 'do theology'.[2] In the course of the *De Veritate* one or two Scriptural quotations are brought in to show how a word should be used, but that is all. There is no exhaustive catalogue of relevant Biblical passages, or corroboration from the Fathers. The student is to make the connections for himself when he reads, and apply a method not a mass of parallels to the analysis of the text.

This, then, is the regular practice of the teaching which underlies the *Monologion* and Anselm's later treatises, and which prompted Anselm's monks to ask him for a written account of reflections he had evidently shared with them over a long period. He enabled them by this method to feel themselves capable of arriving at some idea of God by straightforward practical use of their experience and their reason, and at the same time never to lose sight of the infinite greatness of God.

II

Anselm demonstrates again and again throughout his writings the primacy of Scripture's authority for him. Almost always, when he has set out a rational argument, he pauses before continuing to illustrate what he has said from Scripture, or rather, to test it against Scripture. In the *De Concordia* (III.6), he explains that nothing which Scripture does not contain, explicitly or implicitly, is conducive to salvation. If reason sometimes leads us to make a statement which cannot be found in so many words in Scripture we must first look to see if it can be proved by reference to Scripture. Even if that is not possible, we can still apply a Scriptural test. If it is clearly reasonable and Scripture in no respect contradicts it, we may infer that it is supported by Scripture's authority, for Scripture leaves no room for error. If Scripture is found to oppose our reasoning, even if that reasoning seemed to us to be unassailable, we must let it go as false. So Scripture contains within it the authority for all truths which may be arrived at by reason. The point is made again in the final sentences of chapter 14 of the *De Processione Spiritus Sancti*.

Reasoning always stands under correction by higher authority (CDH I.2).

Anselm's doctrine of Scripture and reason is of a piece with his theory of a continuous revelation in the community of the Church (CDH, commendation to Pope Urban II). This seems to him both a natural and organic growth, in which revelation to individual minds plays a part (his own certainly not excepted), and a process which obeys formal rules within the Church's structure. In matters of decision-making in doctrine, Anselm held that the local Church 'extended throughout a single kingdom' is within its rights to establish in liturgical usage that which is in accordance with right faith. Thus it was perfectly proper for the *Filioque* clause to be added to the Creed in the nations and kingdoms which used the Latin language (Pr 13). It is also possible for larger units to be thought of as local Churches. At the end of his treatise on the Procession of the Holy Spirit Anselm is conscious that because the work was commissioned at the Council of Bari it is likely to be read as something of an official statement, on the part of what may be called the 'Latin Church', and he is careful to insist that any errors it may prove to contain are to be attributed to him personally and not to the judgement of the Latin Church.

The ecclesial identity of such units is closely bound up with the authority of the episcopacy. Anselm takes it for granted that any settlement of the *Filioque* question in earlier times as now would necessitate a meeting of Latin Bishops with Greek Bishops in Council (Pr 13). The common consent of bishops is essential if the decrees or canons of any Council are to carry official status. Anselm wrote to the Archdeacon of Canterbury about 1102−03 concerning the decrees of the Council of London. He is unwilling to publish them yet, because at the Council itself they were necessarily rather hastily framed and therefore need polishing and perhaps changing. When that has been done they must receive the common consent (*communis consensus*) of Anselm's fellow-bishops (*coepiscopi*) (Letter 257).

Disciplinary decisions of Councils ought to be obeyed. Herbert, bishop of Thetford is instructed to expel from their benefices those clergy who are refusing to submit to the ruling of the Council of London that they should put away their wives and live as celibates (Letter 254).

III

How is it possible for a creature, provided by God with good working senses, to misperceive the reality of created things? If I look through coloured glass, I think what I see is the colour of the glass. If I look through plain glass, I think the glass is the colour of whatever lies on the opposite side. If a child looks at a statue of a dragon, he is frightened of it, although his senses tell him exactly what an adult's senses would tell him, and the adult is not afraid. But even an adult, looking at a stick standing upright in a pool of water so that the end sticks out, may think the stick is broken when it is not (because of the effect of refraction). The fault lies, says Anselm, not in the senses nor in the things perceived, which are all true to themselves as God's creations, but in the human judgement (V 6).

Here we see him exploring for himself some of the implications of the Augustinian theory of signs which underlies all his treatment of language. Augustine held that God makes provision in both 'things' perceived by the senses and words, for pointing us to divine realities which we could not otherwise begin to grasp.[3] In the *De Doctrina Christiana* and the *De Magistro* he works out a theory which lays great emphasis upon the principle that words exist to communicate or 'signify' and which thus ties in with the preoccupations of logico-grammarians in Anselm's day, and for several generations after, with the manner in which words point to or stand for things.[4] As early as the *De Grammatico* and the *De Veritate* Anselm was wrestling with the relation between words and propositions and the things they signify, and with the deeper epistemological questions of the relation in which these acts of signifying stand to the speaker and the listener and their knowledge of things.

Anselm's philosophical and theological method was rooted in the skills in logic and language which he had learned as a young man, and it remained so. The importance of these technical principles will be apparent again and again as we go on, and we must pause over them for a moment here. Sometimes the technicalities are straightforward enough, and might be found in the simplest textbook. He points out, for example, that *percussio*, a beating, is derived from the past participle of *percutere* and therefore from a passive form. But we use it with an active signification (V 8). This sort of alertness to the grammatical structure of language frequently stands him in good stead in problem-solving. In this instance, he is anxious to show how active and passive may both be present in ideas of 'ought'. That is to say, it is possible to understand that Christ was both under an obligation to suffer death and under no obligation. He did what he 'ought', but he was not compelled.

In only one of his treatises did Anselm take a purely logical and grammatical problem as his theme. He includes this *De Grammatico* with the three 'little treatises' which he intended as introductions to the study of Holy Scripture (Preface to *De Veritate*), and its presence among them indicates the importance in his mind of a technical grounding in the liberal arts, for reading the Bible with a proper understanding of the way its language behaves.

In Latin usage a word such as *grammaticus* may function as an adjective ('grammatical' or 'literate') or as a noun ('a grammarian'). In the first case, it seems to denote a quality, in the second a substance. Because Roman grammatical theory does not separate adjectives from nouns among the parts of speech but classifies them as a sub-group of nouns, the difference is not easy to state in the grammatical terms of Anselm's day. There is a logical problem, too. Aristotle (*Categories* VIII 10[a]), and Boethius (*On Aristotle's Categories* III: PL 64, 252), say that something such as *grammaticus* (or *albus*, 'white', and so on) is a quality and not a substance. But if we are thinking about the thing signified by one of these 'denominatives' (*denominativa*) we seem to run into a difficulty:

Every *grammaticus* is a man.
Every man is a substance.

Surely it follows that *grammaticus* must be a substance? That is all right as long as *grammaticus* signifies 'a grammarian'. But it is not all right if *grammaticus* is taken to signify 'grammatical' or 'literate'. 'Literate' is not a substance. This is the problem with which the 'pupil' presents Anselm. It is handled by deploying the basic principles of syllogistic argumentation as well as by marshalling grammatical rules, and Anselm succeeds in generating from what are—by comparison with later mediaeval debates—comparatively basic technical principles, a number of original approaches to finding a solution. [5]

One of his devices deployed in the *De Grammatico* and elsewhere echoes the Augustinian theme of the difference between 'common usage' (*usus loquendi, consuetudo loquendi*) and both 'proper', or technically exact usage and the special usages of Biblical language. These are perhaps the most important notions about language which Anselm brings to problem-solving in the study of Scripture, that is, to the interpretation of texts which appear to present grammatical or logical anomalies. In *De Concordia* II.2, for example, we find a reference to 'propriety' of usage. We pray that God will not lead us into temptation, but that is strictly an improper use of language, for we certainly do not mean that God might deliberately lead us into evil; what we are saying is that we hope to be delivered from temptation. It would be grammatically more 'proper' to speak of God's refraining from correcting us when we find ourselves tempted. Similarly, 'fore-knowledge' and 'pre-destination' are not strictly 'proper' usages, for nothing is present to God 'earlier' or 'later'; all things are present to him 'now' (*ibid.*).

When the Bible uses tenses it does so interchangeably, for it refers to time in the context of eternity (C I.5). When Paul says that God foreknew, predestined, called, justified and glorified whom he would, all these things must be understood as taking place in an eternal present before God, for in eternity everything is simultaneous (*ibid.*). It was with the deliberate intention of making it clear that he was not speaking of events in time that the Apostle chose to use the past tense, even of events which are, temporally speaking, in the future. He had to do so, because there is no way of signifying the eternal present with the tenses we have at our disposal in human language. So we must understand that when Scripture speaks as though what is done by free choice is necessary, it is speaking in accordance with the laws of eternity, where all truth (and only truth) is present immutably (*ibid.*). The use of words for 'willing' and for the Father's actions towards the Son in a number of Gospel and Epistle passages are scrupulously analysed in the *Cur Deus Homo* so as to show that again human language is doing its best to accommodate a higher reality and its usages are being adapted to express as far as it is possible for them to do so, truths which are really beyond their compass (e.g. CDH I.10).

Anselm learned his definitional method from Porphyry's *Isagoge*, with the Boethian commentary which made it a standard textbook for beginners in·logic in the mediaeval period, and from Cicero's *Topica* and (probably) Marius Victorinus's *De Definitione*. The approach is to classify first broadly, and then increasingly narrowly, so that in the end the thing defined is pinpointed exactly by a definition which, as Anselm describes it, is neither too wide nor too narrow (V II). In his own definitions of truth and justice he was confronting a much more difficult task than that of defining, say, a rabbit, where one can begin by describing it as an animal and go on to specify its distinctive features. But he succeeds in distinguishing two classes of things, those which have 'rightness' (*rectitudo*) and are as they ought to be; and those which lack 'rightness'. Truth clearly belongs to the former class. He investigates all the kinds of *rectitudo* which actions may have, and so on, and which are perceptible to the senses; he is able to conclude by narrowing the classification down, that truth is, strictly, that rightness which only the mind can perceive (V 11). The pupil leads him on to the question of 'justice' by saying that it seems to him that justice is the same thing as rightness. Anselm points out to him, still classifying, that we do not normally say that a stone is 'just' when it does what it ought and falls to the ground when dropped; but we call a man 'just' when he does what he ought. So justice has something to do with willing rightly. But that is not an adequate definition, for it would cover the case of a thief who is compelled to give back what he has stolen. He is willing to do so (rather than be punished), but we do not praise him and call him 'just' for this right willing. The key element in the definition of justice is that it is willing the right for its own sake (V 12). We see Anselm here using the definitional skills he had learned from his formal training in logic creatively, and in a way which makes them a real practical help to the philosopher, as well as to the reader of Scripture.

IV

Certain themes emerge again and again from Anselm's experiments in problem-solving with the aid of this technical equipment. From the 'three treatises pertaining to the study of Holy Scripture' he drew out a theory of 'being as one ought'. In this consist uprightness and correctness and truth and righteousness alike. In the *De Concordia* at the end of his life he asserts that being as we ought is what saves us (I.6); the theme could scarcely be more important to Anselm's doctrine of man and angel, or to his account of the work of Christ, or more consistently of use to him throughout a lifetime's work. *De Concordia* III. 3–7 leads on from the 'three treatises' without a ripple.

A few fragments survive of a philosophical discussion which, had it been completed, would have been closer in its subject-matter to the *De Grammatico* in some respects than to any of Anselm's other works, because it deals strictly with technicalities of language. But it is concerned with Anselmian themes which suggest that it may be a much later piece. The pupil asks Anselm to clarify for him concepts Anselm lists at the beginning of the *Cur Deus Homo* (CDH I.1).[6] This complex of 'will, power, and necessity' reappears in many places in Anselm's treatises, as we shall see; but only in the *Cur Deus Homo* and the Philosophical Fragments is it addressed at length; and in the *Cur Deus Homo* it is agreed that its full treatment must be held over for another occasion because it would bulk too large in proportion to what is to follow if it were dealt with at length at the outset. In the Philosophical Fragments the issues are divided into questions about (i) ability or capacity and the lack of these, (ii) possibility and impossibility, (iii) freedom and necessity. The emphasis is upon the ways language is typically used to convey these notions. The pupil has been puzzled by the way we sometimes speak of something being 'able' even though we know it has no ability. If I say that something which does not exist 'can' exist, I am using *posse*, 'to be able', in this way. Anselm often had occasion in his treatises to point to examples of such usages. In the treatise on the fall of Satan, for example, he says that we frequently transfer 'able' or 'unable' from the true source of power or impotence to something else which is not really 'able' at all. If I say, 'a book can be written by me', it is my power I speak of, although the verb is used of the book (Ca 12). In the *De Libertate Arbitrii* we are given a list of such misplaced usages in connection with 'being against one's will' (L 5). In the Philosophical Fragments Anselm begins his explanation by examining the word *facere*, 'to do'. We use it, he notes, not only for actions, but in place of almost every other verb (cf. V 5). We can see this clearly if we consider the possible answers to the question 'What is he doing?'. I might say, 'He is singing', 'He is writing', or 'He is in church', 'He is living as a good man should'. We can even use 'to do' for a negative case where it might seem that 'not-doing' is involved. He who does not love virtue 'does wickedly'; he who does not do what he ought not to do 'does rightly'.

Alongside talk of 'ought' and the analysis of will, power and necessity, in both of which questions of usage (and especially of Scriptural usage) and grammatical and logical considerations loom large, we consistently find reflections on 'right order'. This was a notion which seemed to Anselm cardinal to any understanding not only of the 'natural' order and of 'political' order, but also of the ordering of thought. It belongs with *convenientia* and *decentia*, harmony and fittingness, in his scheme of proving. That is to say, Anselm held that what fits that which we know or hold by faith is likely to be right.

To see this 'doing what one ought' as a narrow or life-denying concept would be fundamentally to misunderstand it. Although

Anselm saw conformity to the rules of right order as the absolute duty of men and women, duty was not for him a matter of doing what one ought as opposed to what one wanted to do. To be and do that for which one was created was, for any rational creature, freedom and delight. The alternative was always to be chafing at restrictions felt as such only because one's will was at cross-purposes with the will of God. Will, power and necessity, right order, and the ideas of owing and ought all come together here. Anselm never states the theory on which all this rests as a whole, but it is implicitly footnoted everywhere in his writings. It is the rationale of all his thinking. It is also original to Anselm in its formulation. Augustine has a great deal to say in his writing on evil about the disorderliness of thought and behaviour which results from sin, but he lacked the concepts Anselm was able to draw from his experience of a differently ordered secular world, and Anselm's natural bent for abstractions. (Augustine says in the *Confessions* that he found the greatest difficulty in grasping the idea of the soul as 'spiritual'; his mind kept coming back to the notion of very fine matter.) The natural bent for abstractions gave Anselm insights into the interplay of forces between 'power' and 'necessity' and the ways in which divine and human will may be seen to interlock with them. Feudal society, improbably enough, gave him patterns of right ordering, not necessarily because it was itself rightly ordered (though Anselm did not question that), but because it was a system which placed every authority in a relatively clear relationship to every other (despite leaving a vexed area over the relation of Church and State) and demonstrated that structure tends to preserve, or even creates harmony. The distress Anselm felt when his relations with the monarch broke down arose in no small measure from the breakdown of the relationship between spiritual and secular jurisdiction within this structure. Anselm's supreme achievement is perhaps to have brought out of the unpromising material of the philosophical and political ideas available to him so elegant and satisfactory a guiding principle for problem-solving.

Notes

1   A possible exception is Chalcidius's commentary on Plato's *Timaeus*, which seems to have had some contemporary circulation.

2   Anselm would have seen *philosophia* as closely allied to *theologia*, as it was for Boethius; *theologia* was not yet in standard use as a term embracing the whole span of what we should now call Christian theology but, as in Boethius's usage, covered principally those aspects of the existence of God and the attributes of the divine nature, Trinity and creation which can be explored by reasoning and which were also examined by ancient philosophers.

3   A useful introduction is M. Colish, *The Mirror of Language* (Yale, 1967).

4   *The Cambridge History of Later Mediaeval Philosophy*, ed. A. Kenny, N. Kretzmann, J. Pinborg (Cambridge, 1982) gives reliable coverage of the *status quaestionis*.

5   See D. P. Henry, *The De Grammatico* (Dordrecht, 1974).

6   cf. II.17 and L 12; Ca 12; I 16; Preface to M.

4

The being of God

I

In the *Monologion* we see Anselm much influenced by his reading of Augustine. His subject is the divine being in its unity and Trinity. He explores the nature of God, attributes of the Godhead as supremely good, beautiful, merciful, just, omnipotent and omniscient, on assumptions shot through with Augustinian Platonism. He discusses the idea of language in its relation to God as Creator, in terms of the motifs of idea, or form, and matter. When he comes to the Trinity, he borrows from Augustine's *De Trinitate* the image of the Trinity to be found in the mind of man, in the distinctness of memory, intellect and will within a single being. But the long series of chapters in which he unfolds all this left him dissatisfied. He does not say that they seemed to him derivative, but perhaps they did; certainly they struck him as untidy, as forming a chain of arguments. We must not overstate this dissatisfaction. Anselm made no attempt to withdraw copies of the treatise from circulation, and when, after a long silence, Lanfranc was persuaded to send him his comments and found fault with the work, Anselm made, as far as the manuscript evidence tells us, no changes. He was content with the work as it stood because it could be said to have fulfilled its purpose. It was intended, he says, as 'an example of meditating on faith by reason (*meditandi de ratione fidei*)'; in it, by silent reasoning (*tacite secum ratiocinando*), the mind explores the unknown (*quae nesciat*) (P, *Proemium*). But it left him with an idea for another kind of book.

'I began to wonder whether a single argument might be found which would need no other to support it', he says. This was to be an argument to prove that God exists and that he is the Supreme Good,

49

needing none but himself; the source of all creation; and at the same time to prove all the other things we believe about him (P, *Proemium*). In the event, the single *argumentum* was not allowed to stand alone. The devotional context of meditation which Anselm envisaged as the setting of the *Monologion* here takes the form of passages of stylistically quite distinct devotional writing, full of the assonance and alliteration, the climax and paradox and antithesis of the prayers and meditations, which introduce the work and form a frame for its arguments throughout. But the keynote of the central and unique argument was to be its elegance and its independence, its self-evidency and simplicity.

It did not prove easy to find. We have accounts of the search both from Anselm himself, in his preface to the *Proslogion*, and from his biographer Eadmer, who tells the story as it was remembered by Anselm himself and perhaps by some of the monks of Bec who were there. Anselm became preoccupied, distracted in chapel, unable to concentrate upon spiritual or practical duties, until he began to think that the idea of finding such an argument was a temptation of the Devil and he had better give it up. But he found that the idea pressed itself upon him, as from behind a curtain, more and more as he resisted it. There came a moment when he grasped it, and experienced a great sense of joy and release. It seemed to him then that it was important to try to communicate it, so that others could share his pleasure (*Proemium*).

The *Proslogion* opens with an invitation:

> Come, now , little man, come away from your duties for a little while, and hide for a space from your tumultuous thoughts. . . . Give yourself up to God and rest for a time in him. Enter the chamber of your mind and shut out everything but God and what helps you to seek him, and with the door closed, seek him out.

The quest is to be spiritual as well as intellectual. Anselm dwells at some length on the fundamental paradoxes of man's experience of God, the yearning and the frustration of finding that that which he seeks is beyond his understanding; the light which is God's dwelling place but which, instead of illuminating him to us, presents an inaccessible and dazzling brightness; the loss of that for which man was made which makes it impossible now for him to be himself. He calls for help in his quest and he goes forward in faith. Then the second chapter opens with a philosophical argument which takes its starting-point from Scripture, the Fool who has said in his heart that there is no God (Psalm 13/14:1; 52/53:1), but which goes on in a manner stylistically stripped down, and bare of all but the bones of the reasoning.

God is, we believe, that than which no greater can be thought. Even the Fool understands those words when he hears them, and so it must be conceded that that 'something than which nothing greater can be thought' exists at least in his mind. But it is not the same to exist in the mind and actually to exist. A painter planning a picture has it in his mind, but it does not exist until he has painted it. That which exists in reality (*in re*) as well as in thought (*in intellectu*) is obviously greater than that which exists only in the mind. If God existed only in the mind, it would be possible to conceive of a greater than he, who existed in reality as well, and then that which we have defined as 'That than which nothing greater can be thought' would not be 'That than which nothing greater can be thought'. Anselm draws the conclusion that 'That than which nothing greater can be thought' must therefore exist in reality.

It is here, in this last step, that those who have failed to be convinced by the 'ontological argument' for the existence of God, as it has come to be called, point to the likelihood that some sleight of hand has been practised. Gaunilo, a monk of Marmoutiers, of whom we know nothing more, wrote a shrewd riposte, suggesting that Anselm's argument could be used to prove the existence in reality of many fantasies of the mind, for example, of the most beautiful island which can be conceived. Anselm replied that his argument has force only in the unique case of God, who stands at the height of all things which we may conceive of (but he was sufficiently pleased with the comment to instruct that Gaunilo's reply on behalf of the Fool and his own answer to it should thereafter always be copied with the main text of the *Proslogion*). Aquinas dismissed the argument on the ground that it amounts to saying that the very definition of God entails his existence. More recent critics have sometimes not fully allowed for the world of thought in which the argument lies for Anselm. The devotional content of the first chapter is not merely a device for creating an appropriate mood, a suitable attitude of mind. It is intellectually as well as spiritually a setting for the argument itself. The 'heart' (*cor*) in which the Fool speaks to himself, and in which the *intellectus* of chapter II is lodged, is the seat of thought and feeling alike in the Old Testament, the place where faith and understanding come together. Although Anselm did not see the argument as presupposing faith, he himself approached it in faith, and his Augustinian and Platonic heritage made it natural for him to think of reality as primarily a property or attribute of that which is most highly abstract and spiritual and only secondarily attaching to the concrete and particular exemplifications of it which we should now be inclined to call 'real'. The movement from existence in thought to existence in reality as it refers to God—and that is an important proviso, as Anselm says to Gaunilo—is therefore conceived of as taking place in a realm of thought which is itself the supreme reality. At the same time the assent the argument commands is simultaneously an assent of faith and of reason.

There can be no doubt of the originality of this argument. All the other proofs for the existence of God catalogued by Aquinas and developed in later centuries are in one form or other inferences from the evidences of the presence of a Creator behind the structures and objects of the world. They proceed from effects back to a Cause. Anselm's argument rests upon a conception of the very Being of God as intellectually necessary in itself, and from it he is indeed able to draw many of the further proofs he hoped for, of the attributes of God and so on.

II

Before we go on to these, we need to pause for a moment over the arguments of chapters III and IV. Here Anselm, seeking to reinforce the argument of chapter II, explores the notion that such a Being cannot even be thought not to exist. What cannot be thought not to exist must be greater than what can be thought not to exist (if being and greatness are as intimately united as they certainly are in Anselm's Platonism). But it seems (chapter IV) that the Fool has done the impossible. He has 'said in his heart' what cannot be thought. We must distinguish, says Anselm, between thinking which involves bringing the words in question to mind, and thinking which grasps the thing which the words signify. In the first sense, and only in that sense, can God be thought not to exist. The Fool thought the words, but he did not understand their meaning. The words held for him either no signification at all, or a peculiar signification of some sort (*aliqua extranea significatio*). Had he understood their true meaning, he could not have thought them.

The talk of signification in chapter IV of the *Proslogion* is of the first importance in understanding the theory of language held by Anselm and, with increasing technical sophistication and refinement, by his scholastic successors. The relationship of signification is a complex one. A single word may have many potential significations, or 'dictionary definitions', but only one signification (properly 'supposition') in a particular context. It is essential to clear thinking and useful argument to recognize correctly the signification which applies in a particular proposition. Significations may also be 'transferred' so that they become figurative, as when we call a brave man a lion without confusing him with a four-footed beast. Anselm's point here is that signification is detachable from what is signified. The Fool may think words without necessarily thinking of their proper significations. He may think empty words, or words used in some other sense.

In the remainder of the chapters of the *Proslogion*, Anselm investigates the implications of his *argumentum* (the notion that God is greater than anything else which can be thought). This is used in the Ciceronian way as a 'seat of argument', a *locus* or paradigm from which a series of arguments can be drawn (cf. Cicero, *Topica* II.8). To be greater than anything else which can be thought is to be the Supreme Good. That is to be the Good through which every other good exists (a main theme of the *Monologion*), and thus the Creator of all things from nothing (chapter V). It is better to be *sensibilis*, capable of perception; omnipotent; merciful; impassible, than not to be so, and so we know that God must be all these things (chapter VI). Anselm throws up in delight a series of paradoxes which he proceeds to resolve. How can God perceive if he is not a body? To perceive is to know. In human beings perception takes place through the senses, but God knows all things directly and so indeed he perceives. How can God be omnipotent if there are things he cannot do (for God cannot lie)? But to be able to lie is not a power but an impotence, and the more one lies the more one is in the thralls of 'adversity and perversity'. To say that a person 'can lie' is in fact to misuse the words. The 'can' signifies not power but impotence, as when we say to someone who denies that something exists, 'It is as you say it is', when we really mean 'It is not as you say it is not' (chapter VII). How can God be both merciful and incapable of suffering? When God shows mercy we 'feel' the effects of it, but he himself does not suffer pains in his compassion, says Anselm. How can it be just for God to spare the wicked? It is better to be good to both good and wicked than to be good to the good alone, and so it cannot be incompatible with God's justice for him to be merciful. But it is also just for God to punish the wicked. How is that compatible with the justice of his sparing them? Just as in seeking to understand his mercy we must distinguish mercy in relation to ourselves from mercy felt by God, so in the case of justice, we must understand that God is just in relation to himself and not in relation to the deserts of the wicked when he spares those he might justly punish. How is God alone limitless and eternal, when other spirits are also limitless (*incircumscripti*) and eternal (*aeterni*)? God alone is without beginning. Other boundless and immortal spirits, the angels and mankind, are without end but not without a beginning (chapter XIII).

III

These matters resolved, Anselm asks 'My soul, have you found what you were seeking?' He gathers up his conclusions and begins to press systematically onwards into the 'inaccessible light'. God is not only that than which nothing greater can be thought. He is greater still. When we have said this of him we have only touched the hem of what he is. Anselm now perceives that this axiom is itself in a way the inaccessible light in which God dwells, because as we contemplate it we are dazzled and our understanding falls back, dazed by its inability to penetrate further. Now the thought becomes mingled with imagery. God is harmony, fragrance, sweetness, softness, beauty, and yet the soul smells and does not detect God's fragrance, tastes and has no perception of the savour of God, feels and cannot sense his softness. To consider God's attributes separately, his goodness, life, wisdom and so on, leads us nowhere, for he is not the sum of parts (chapters XVII–XVIII). God is not contained in anything, in today or tomorrow; he himself contains all things, and so although we have piecemeal and limited ways of attaining to an understanding or a knowledge of God, they will not be of any use to us in the end. Anselm seems in the last chapters of the *Proslogion* to throw aside all the advice he had given and was consistently to give again, to his monks and his wider readership, to take human experience as a starting-point. He stretches for the prize of a single, unitary apperception of God as he is, the supreme goal of his search for the single *argumentum* which was to have not only intellectual elegance but spiritual power.

The Trinitarian material which takes up a good deal of space in the *Monologion* has only a brief mention here. Chapter XXIII underlines that the good which is God is equally Father, Son and Holy Spirit. More important is the fresh material on the enjoyment of the good with its sketch of a heaven more intensely and personally realized than anything Augustine affords in the final chapters of the *De Civitate Dei.* Anselm describes a joy and satisfaction which will be anything but generalized and which is anything but dull. Each of the redeemed is to have in its fullness what gave him most delight in this life. He will share it with the whole company of heaven in a way which will double and redouble the joy of each:

> Surely if someone you really loved as yourself possessed the same blessedness, your own joy would be double, for you would rejoice for him as much as for yourself. If two, or three or many more possessed it, you would rejoice so many times the more. So in that perfect and pure love of the countless holy angels and holy men, where the love of one's neighbour will be perfect, . . . the heart will scarcely be able to grasp its joy.

And when we add to that the incomparably greater love each will have for God, we can see that an immeasurably greater gladness will be enjoyed in that (chapter XXV).

Nowhere else in his writings does Anselm reach a peak of joyous affirmation like this. It is the apotheosis of the fusion of prayer and thought in the framing of the *Proslogion* argument and its derivatives. The final chapter returns us to more familiar ground, as Anselm sinks back a little into longing and striving for that which has just been so vividly present to him. But he has brought his understanding of the being of God into the one context in which it can be enjoyed in fullness of experience; he has envisaged the absoluteness of the mutual love of the community of friends; he has seen heaven in a way mystical writers have rarely done, as a shared experience of a multitude of souls and not the solitary brief rapture of one individual.

Anselm's is a towering God, whose unimaginable height of Being is, in a sense, the very thing that makes us know he is there. He saw no need to try to bring down to human level in his thinking a God beyond human comprehension, or indeed any possibility of it. That is worth emphasizing, because it contrasts with some recent theological trends. Anselm saw clearly that Christ is God making himself approachable, and that that entirely 'reachable' Jesus does the necessary work of making a bridge; the Prayer to Christ shows Anselm in loving talk with him as a friend. This is worth emphasizing because it is a central importance to Anselm's thinking that this contrast between God in his humanity and God in his divinity should be strong. For Anselm, it makes Christ's coming among men more human, not less, and underlines for him how wholly Christ was man.

5

Trinity

I

We see less of the influence of the mediaeval ideas of order and the little illustrations from everyday life, and more of metaphysics in the *De Incarnatione Verbi* and the *De Processione Spiritus Sancti*. The two works were written in quite different circumstances and some years apart, but they deal with aspects of the same question of the relationship of the threeness of the Persons to the oneness of God.

In the *Monologion* Anselm's principal debt is to Augustine's *De Trinitate*, with its images of the Trinity in the mind of man put there by the Creator to help his creatures approach the mystery of his being in their own understanding. But here his borrowings are chiefly from Boethius, both the theological tractates and the works on Aristotle. Boethius's *theologia* spans much the same range as that of pagan philosophers: dealing with questions of the nature and attributes of God which lend themselves to discussion by the procedures of formal reasoning. Boethius considers in particular the ways in which Aristotle's ten Categories may be predicated of God, and shows, in the Augustinian way, that all but 'relation' are subsumed in 'substance'. That is to say, where we call a creature 'large', 'kind', 'active', 'here', 'now', and so on, knowing that these attributes may be altered without the substance of the creature changing, in the case of God to say that he is 'merciful' or 'just' or 'omnipotent' is not to speak of a mutable quality. God is not only merciful; he is mercy, and so on. His attributes are his very being. The sole exception is the relation between Father and Son, Son and Holy Spirit, Father and Holy Spirit. We cannot here say that the Father is the Son as we can say that God's justice is also his mercy. A relationship exists. It is unique among relationships in that it is absolute and eternal and of the very being of God. If I am a father and you are my son, that is a state of affairs which had a beginning. I did not always have a son. But the Father always had a Son. If I am a master and you are my servant, that is a state of affairs which can change; I may make you free. But nothing can ever change in the relationship of Father, Son and Holy Spirit. Thus the Aristotelian categories are profoundly challenged by the paradox of the Trinity, and the minds of Christian thinkers in the tradition largely founded on Augustine and Boethius in the Middle Ages were exercised by the technical problems posed.

Anselm seems to have begun working on the subject after he had completed his own Trinitarian reflections in the *Monologion* and *Proslogion*, because he was forced into it by the debate about Roscelin's contention that Anselm himself had implied either the three Persons are three 'things' or the Father and the Spirit were incarnate with the Son.

In a letter to Fulk, bishop of Beauvais, he describes what he has heard that Roscelin is saying (although he finds it hard to believe). These three 'things' exist separately like three angels, united by the will and power they share. So if custom or usage allowed, it would be correct to speak of three Gods. If, as Anselm is told, a Council is to be held at Rheims in the near future to settle the matter, he asks Fulk to speak for him, and defend him against Roscelin's misrepresentation of his position. Roscelin includes Lanfranc with Anselm in his attack, and Anselm instructs Fulk to say that no such accusation was ever made against Lanfranc when he was alive, that his holiness of life completely exonerates him, and that no fresh accusation can now be made after his death. For himself, he affirms his faith in the Creeds. In a letter to the monk John he goes a little further into the technicalities of what Roscelin seems to have been saying. His chief concern is with the problems raised by the first of Roscelin's alternatives: that the Persons are three distinct 'things'. Anselm perceives a good deal of muddle in Roscelin's arguments. If he is saying that the three relations in which the Persons stand are three things, no one will argue with him, provided we are careful to define what kind of 'things' they are. But if he wants to say these 'things' are Gods, he does not understand what he is saying.

The Council was duly held and Roscelin abjured his error. Anselm stopped work on the open letter he had been writing because he thought everyone understood that what Roscelin had said was false, and there was therefore no need for it. But later, when he was archbishop, he heard that Roscelin had begun to say the same things again, and to claim that he had first abjured his words only because he was afraid of being killed by the angry mob. Some of Anselm's monks begged him to solve the problem and publish a book. He insists that he has done so only because they have asked him and not because he thinks that the faith needs support from him any more than Mount Olympus would do were he to labour industriously round it with ropes and pegs to ensure that it did not fall down. It certainly seems to be the case that Anselm had no inward urge to write on the topic. There is none of the passionate longing to find a solution which drove him on in writing the *Proslogion*; nor did this book arise, like the *Monologion* and the treatises on studying Scripture, out of conversations with his brothers (I 1). Indeed, he includes in his prefatory letter to Urban strong words on the importance of employing reason in the service of faith and not to challenge it. The Christian ought to hold his faith constantly, loving it and living it, and in that spirit do his best to discover with his reason why it is true. But if his reason cannot bring him to understanding, he should not toss his horns like a quarrelsome beast, but bow his head in reverence before the mystery (I 1).

II

In the uncompleted first version of the *De Incarnatione Verbi* which some of his brothers copied and circulated without Anselm's knowledge, he had concentrated upon showing the absurdity of the first of Roscelin's alternatives: that the three Persons are three 'things', in a way which makes them really three Gods. There he had attempted to explain the technical errors in Roscelin's interpretation of the image of the Persons Anselm himself had used and drawn from grammar and logic. (We might say that God is Father and Son in rather the way that we say that a man is 'white' and 'just', and so on, where 'white' and 'just' are denominatives which also signify 'a white man', 'a just man'; but, as Anselm insists, that is no more than a rough comparison, since the divine substance is different from all other substance not only in itself but in the manner in which we can speak of it.) The attempt had failed because it had simply set Roscelin off in further endeavours to prove himself a better technician than Anselm, and thus brought him to further confusion. Now Anselm wanted to be as clear and simple and untechnical as possible. He proposes to take just Father and Son for purposes of discussion.

Whatever can be said of them must also apply to the Holy Spirit as a Person, and there can be no muddle over naming in the case of Father and Son. (Since both Father and Son are 'holy' and are 'spirit', there is room for confusion in the nomenclature which must be used for the Holy Spirit: I 2.)

The first task is to determine what Roscelin can mean by 'two things'. We believe, explains Anselm, that each of the Persons is both that which is peculiar ('proper') to himself and that which is common to all the Persons as God. When we use the word 'God' we understand it to signify that which is common to all the persons, such as omnipotence, eternity. When we use the words 'Father', 'Son', we understand the *res* unique to each, for example, 'begetter', 'the one who is begotten'. The reference here is to the entirely familiar tradition of discussion of the relationship of signification which obtains between *res* and *verbum* which is to be found in Augustine and in Aristotle—Boethius. Which *res* or 'thing' does Roscelin mean when he says that the two Persons are two 'things'? If he means that they are two 'things' in respect to that which is proper to each, every Christian would agree with him. So long as we understand that in calling the Persons 'Father' and 'Son' we are predicating a relation which is not that of one being to another (as would be the case in a human father and son), so not of two substances, there can be no objection to saying that Father and Son are two things (i.e. relations) (I 2). Roscelin had compared these three 'things' which are Persons to three angels. That is again a mistake in predication, Anselm explains. 'Two angels' or 'two souls' are not expressions predicated of what is numerically one and the same. But God is one in number as he is in nature or substance, and so though 'Father' and 'Son' are two, they are predicated of a single substance which is God (I 2). This neatly sidesteps the implicit appeal to the *Proslogion* argument, that if God is composed of three things and is therefore not a simple nature, either no nature is simple, or there is some other nature which in some respect is more excellent than the nature of God (I 4).

III

Anselm now moves on to the other assertion Roscelin has been making: that if Father and Son are not distinct 'things' then the Father (and the Holy Spirit) must have been incarnate with the Son. The Son assumed a human nature into unity with his Person and not into unity with his nature (I 9). Thus he was one and the same Person with the man (*homo*) he assumed. This alone shows that the Father and the Holy Spirit could not have been incarnate with him, for by definition they could not all become one and the same Person with that one man without becoming one and the same Person with one another and with the Person of the Son (I 9). Moreover, manifest absurdities would follow. If the Holy Spirit had been incarnate he would have been the son of the Virgin, and thus there would have been two 'sons' in the Trinity. There would be inequality in their sonship, for one would be the Son of the Father and the other the son only of a human being. If the Father had become the Virgin's son, there would have been two 'grandsons' in the Trinity. The Father would be the grandson of the parents of the Virgin and his Son would be the grandson of the Virgin (as well as her Son) (I 10).

Anselm supplies an image of the Trinity as a final aid to those who wish to understand the matter clearly, an image of patristic origins and found in Augustine, of a watercourse consisting of spring, river and pool. The Father is the spring, the Son the river, the Spirit the pool. Through all three flows the same water (I 13).

IV

In his treatise *On the Procession of the Holy Spirit*, written as a result of Urban's request at the Council of Bari, Anselm takes up again a number of these arguments and images. He was of course addressing himself to minds which shared the Western academic tradition to only a limited extent; the nascent scholasticism of Anselm's approach is not wholly in tune with Eastern spirituality.

Anselm proceeds in his characteristic way to try to win over the Greeks by the sheer reasonableness of what he has to say. He reviews their common starting-point with Western Christians. Both revere the Gospels. Both believe in all respects but this one, exactly the same things about the one God who is a Trinity. Here Anselm unfolds his own doctrine of the Trinity more fully and in a more relaxed way than he was able to do in the contentious circumstances of writing the *De Incarnatione Verbi*, where some of his points here were under attack.

The Greeks believe like the Latin Christians that God is one and unique and perfect; that he has no parts; and that he is, as a whole, whatever he is. They also believe that he is Father, Son and Holy Spirit. Anselm is now able to express what is understood by this in the terms of 'naming', and 'signification' without the oppressive shadow of Roscelin's objections looking over his shoulder. 'Father' and 'Son' do not signify the same as the word 'God'; nevertheless if we speak of 'Father' and 'Son', or any other two Persons together, or of the Persons one at a time, or of all three Persons at once, we refer to a single God, whole and perfect.

Anselm introduces at this stage a shared belief of Greeks and Latins about the relationship which the Holy Spirit bears to the Father and the Son. The Holy Spirit is the spirit of the Father and of the Son. There is no difference of opinion, either, about the manner in which God exists from God in the case of Son and Holy Spirit respectively. The Son exists from the Father by being begotten. The Holy Spirit exists from the Father by proceeding. In both cases we understand that this means that what the Son is he has from the Father, and what the Holy Spirit is he has from the Father, but that this takes place in two distinct ways (by begetting and by proceeding). These relational differences are implied in the naming of the Persons. When we speak of the Father we understand him to be someone who begets. When we speak of the Son we understand him to be someone who is begotten. When we speak of the Holy Spirit we understand him to be someone who proceeds. And we accept that the Fatherhood and Sonship and 'being the Spirit of' applies uniquely to the relationships which obtain between the Persons of the Godhead. So there can be no Father in the Trinity but the Father of the Son, no Son except of the Father, and the Holy Spirit is the Spirit of no one except the Father and the Son.

This brings Anselm to the notion of 'relation'. It is the difference of relation in which the distinction of the Persons primarily consists he says. When a substance has its existence from a substance and we name the two in accordance with the relation of 'existing from', we arrive at an immutable difference. For example, a father cannot be his son, or a son his father. In the case of the Trinity, whose relationships do not spill over to other persons, there is no possibility that the son of a father may be himself the father of someone else.

Anselm still needs to establish one or two principles in order to make his case. The Holy Spirit exists from the Father—that is not in dispute. But we can also say that he does not exist from himself because it is impossible for the same being to exist from himself and to exist from another. We can go further and make this claim: 'Either the Son exists from the Holy Spirit, or the Holy Spirit exists from the Son'. To deny this claim is to say that there is not only one God; or that the Son is not God; or that the Holy Spirit is not

God; or that God does not exist from God, and all these have been freely conceded by Greeks as well as Latins. Now if we can show that the Son does not exist from the Holy Spirit, it must follow that the Holy Spirit exists from the Son, and that is what is at issue.

Anselm now fields an objection arising out of a topic of considerable general interest in later mediaeval thinking: that of wholes and parts. When God exists from God, it seems that either the whole exists from the whole or a part exists from a part, or else the whole exists from a part or a part exists from a whole. But God has no parts. So the only way in which God can exist from God is as whole from whole. But it seems that if we argue that the Son exists from the whole of God, we must say that he exists from both Father and Holy Spirit; and that likewise the Holy Spirit, if he exists from the whole of God, must exist from both Father and Son. Anselm is here facing a difficulty like the one he confronted in the *De Incarnatione Verbi*, where he must show without prejudice to the unity of Trinity that that which is proper to one Person is not necessarily proper to another. He has already shown that plurality arises in the Trinity from the distinction between the 'begottenness' of the Son and the 'procession' of the Holy Spirit. That plurality obliges us to see an 'existing from' as also operating between Son and Holy Spirit, in order to maintain the harmony of the relationships among the Persons. If the Son existed from the Holy Spirit, a set of anomalies would arise like those we met in the case of incarnation. If by begetting, the Son would then be the son of the Holy Spirit and that would mean that there were two Fathers in the Trinity. If he proceeded from the Holy Spirit he would be the spirit of the Holy Spirit. So neither by proceeding nor by being begotten does the Son exist from the Holy Spirit, and these are the only two means of so existing which are possible for him. Therefore the other option must be the case, and the Holy Spirit must exist from the Son (I 1).

V

But in what way? In the second chapter of his *De Processione Spiritus Sancti* Anselm considers the possibilities. The difference between the Persons goes deeper, Anselm argues, than such matters as having or not having a Son, or proceeding or not proceeding. It has to do with having one's essence from the other. The Holy Spirit is distinct from the Father because he has his essence from him, and for that reason alone. This gives Anselm scope to make a distinction necessary to his case between 'proceeding' and being 'given' or 'sent'. The Holy Spirit proceeds from the Father eternally, as having his being from the Father. But he is given or sent by the Son to creatures. This giving or sending is also eternal in relation to the Holy Spirit himself, although those who receive him experience his being 'given' or 'sent' in time. Now if we say that the Holy Spirit proceeds only by existing from the Father, we must also concede that he exists by proceeding from the Son, because we are simply saying that he is God from God, and the Son too is God. If we say that he proceeds only when he is given or sent to creatures, he certainly proceeds from the Son, who gives and sends him, as well as from the Father. If we say that he proceeds in both ways, we find that he must proceed from the Son in both ways equally.

The case thus made by reasoning is now supported extensively from Scripture. Anselm marshals the key texts which have reference to the Holy Spirit and shows how they endorse his points in detail (Pr 3–7).

We come to objections. It is clear from a comment Anselm allows himself about the mistaken views of one of the bishops he met at Bari that there had been a good deal of heated theological discussion of an informal sort during the Council. Anselm has a fair idea from which directions the objections to his arguments will come, and he fields them boldly and comprehensively. The first two, considered in chapters 8 and 9, concern the 'structure' of the Trinity and make use of two patristic images which Anselm would have known of from his reading of Augustine, and the Greeks from their own Fathers, at least in the first instance. The Trinity is compared to the Sun, from which comes both light and heat. The light and the heat exist equally from the sun. We do not say that the heat exists from the light or the light from the heat. Why can we not say that Son and Holy Spirit exist from the Father in that way? Anselm sees this as implying an inferiority in the Son and the Holy Spirit which he has been at pains to avoid even hinting at in his own account of the matter. There can be no 'lesser' or 'later' in the Trinity. There can be no grades or degrees in God, no intervals such as separate points in geometry to make them into a line. Eternity (and *a fortiori* God himself) is like three *puncta* resting upon one another with no intervals between, he says in the *De Incarnatione Verbi* (I.15), and he returns to the comparison with eternity here. This analogy of the sun and its light and heat, if properly understood, proves to be irrelevant to the argument in hand. The most notable thing about the heat and the brightness is that we cannot distinguish where one begins and the other ends, or tell the sun itself from its heat and brightness, even though we can clearly recognize that the three are different. Thus far and no further is this a helpful analogy in nature to aid our understanding of what the Trinity is (Pr 8).

Similarly, the analogy of the watercourse already used in the *De Incarnatione Verbi* is, Anselm says, pressed further than it will bear by the Greeks. They point to its weakness. The pool which is taken to represent the Holy Spirit seems to proceed from the spring which is the Father somehow 'through' (*per*) the Son. Anselm had learned from his painful experiences with Roscelin that an analogy could be as damaging as it could be helpful if it got into hostile hands, because it could be stretched too far. His own habit was to use such helps to give a brief illumination and something familiar and concrete for his listener or reader to hold on to in the midst of abstraction or a chain of hard reasoning. The Greeks hold up the word 'through' and ask what is the difference between saying that the Spirit proceeds from the Father 'through' the Son and saying that the Father creates 'through' the Word. Anselm has no objection to *per* so long as its implications are properly understood. By all means let us say that, he says, for certainly what has been created by the Father through the Word has been created by the Word himself. Christ himself says, 'Whatever the Father does, the Son does also' (John 5:19). It is in this way that the Holy Spirit proceeds from the Father through the Son. There is no sequence, no subordination of the Son to the Father in this, as would be the case in a watercourse where the stream comes after the spring and the pool after the stream.

VI

There are now some awkwardnesses to be got out of the way. Certain Scriptural texts seem on the face of it to favour the Greeks, and Anselm must account for these if his marshalling of texts in his own favour is to carry weight. Why, for example, did Christ say, 'When the Paraclete comes . . . who proceeds from the Father' and not mention himself too (John 15:26)? That is quite a commonplace habit of his, says Anselm. It was not unusual for him to attribute to the Father alone or to the Spirit alone or to himself alone what is clearly meant to be understood of all three. When he says, 'He who sees me sees the Father also', he implicitly includes the Holy Spirit (John 14:9). What is at issue here is a question of Scriptural usage, a language question, not a question of fact (Pr 9).

The Greeks rightly point out that the *Filioque* clause was a Western addition to a Creed previously accepted by both Eastern and Western Christians; they ask why they were not consulted. Anselm argues that it was a necessary addition and no rational objection prevented its being added. There was no reason for the Latins to think the Greeks would not approve it, and in any case, it would have been almost insuperably difficult to get together the Greek bishops with the Latin for consultation (Pr 13).

Finally, he introduces an argument wholly original and based on the principle of harmony and balance embedded in the notion of *convenientia*. Six differences can be found in the Trinity: having a father, not having a father, having a son, not having a son, having a spirit proceeding from oneself, not having a spirit proceeding from oneself. Each of the Persons has one of these which is peculiar to himself, and by which he differs from the other two Persons. Only the Father has a Son. Only the Son has a Father. Only the Holy Spirit has no one proceeding from him. Each of the Persons has two points of difference which he shares with one other Person. Neither the Father nor the Holy Spirit has a Father. The Son and the Holy Spirit do not have a Son. The Father and the Son have a Spirit proceeding from themselves.

The great strengths of the arguments in the *De Incarnatione Verbi* and the *De Processione Spiritus Sancti* are their mechanical efficiency from a technical point of view and the force of their appeal to criteria of Anselm's day: a reasonableness conceived in an Aristotelian manner, *convenientia* or fittingness, harmony. In attempting to resolve difficulties put to him within this frame of reference (Roscelin's grammatico-logical points, the Greeks' attacks on standard analogies) Anselm does a masterly job.

It is fair criticism to say that the matter and the treatment are dry and limited in scope. We do not discover the Trinity as a wonder. Nor do we learn about the power of love as the binding force in the relationships of the Persons of the Trinity. Some of this Anselm has explored elsewhere. The chapters of the *Monologion* in which he explores the Augustinian imagery of the Trinity in the mind of man take much further the deep notions of the *veritas essentiae*, the truth of being of the Word by which the Supreme Spirit expresses himself (*Monologion* 30 ff.), which he begets and which is his strength and wisdom and so on (M 45) which Anselm examines as a preliminary. Anselm explains how the Father may be understood as memory, the Son as understanding of wisdom of that memory (M 48), and the love with which the Supreme Spirit loves himself as proceeding equally from Father and Son and itself as great as the Supreme Being (M 49–53). He shows how memory, understanding and love are not lacking in any of the Persons, so that one may be said to need the other for remembering, understanding or loving (M 60). All three are one Supreme Being who remembers, understands and loves through himself (M 60). As he contemplates what must baffle reason, Anselm exclaims at its marvellousness and draws back from trying to explain fully what must always dazzle human understanding (M 63–4). He offers, as Augustine had done, in the *De Trinitate* the image of the human mind as divinely appointed mirror of the Trinity (M 67) and experience of loving God as the best way to approach an understanding of his Trinity (M 67), to receive him as reward (M 70). In these last chapters of the *Monologion* Anselm is at his most derivative; he does not take matters far beyond the point Augustine had reached. Did he make any advance on this moderately developed account of the Trinity in writing the *De Incarnatione Verbi* and the *De Processione Spiritus Sancti*? Technically, certainly, and in the originality of his arguments and analogies there is a solid advance. But for the spirituality which accompanies the treatment in the *Monologion* and in the brief chapters of the *Proslogion* which touch on the doctrine of the Trinity, we shall look in vain. Anselm was, in circumstances of controversy in writing the *De Incarnatione Verbi* and the *De Processione Spiritus Sancti*, perhaps inevitably showing in his treatment of these topics the influence of the division between speculative theology and contemplation which was to mark the theology of the later Middle Ages and which is already quite clearly established in the twelfth century.

6

The introduction of sin and evil

We turn now to an area which had already interested Anselm philosophically as well as theologically at the time when he was writing his 'three treatises', and which was to continue to preoccupy him at intervals in his later writings. The problem of evil was not naturally attractive to him in the way the questions of the *Monologion* and *Proslogion* had been. The meditation of these two books on the being and nature of God was prayer as well as theology for Anselm, and it was his nature to prefer to fix his mind on the good and the beautiful and to shut out the negative and the confused.

It was in line with this natural disposition of his mind that Anselm took Augustine's view that evil is nothing,[1] an absence of good. But it was not for that reason of no account; it had to be treated as though (Ca 11) it were a 'something', and a powerful something. Anselm never separates the problem of evil from the problem of sin, for sin partakes of the fearful nothingness of evil. He first tackles the complex of problems raised by this fundamental paradox in the *De Casu Diaboli*. The pupil, who had thought they were coming to the end of their enquiry as Anselm shows that the wicked angels fell because they desired a good which was beyond their natures, begins to perceive that fresh questions are sprouting like suckers from the roots of the questions which have been cut down (Ca 7). What, he asks, was the source of this disordered desire? Desire is nothing but will. If the angels' wills were good, a gift of God, how can they have sinned? If their wills were evil, then God must be the source of evil, for they have nothing they did not receive from their Creator (Ca 1–3). If we try to discover the source in the 'turning' of the will to good or ill we run into the difficulty of explaining why God created so high a creature and made it possible for him to turn away from what he ought to have willed. The ability or capacity which it seems the angels ought to have received was solely that of turning to the good for which they were created (Ca 7). Anselm answers that the evil cannot lie either in the will or in the 'turning' or bending of the will, for these exist and are therefore good gifts of God (Ca 8). He argues that since the good in virtue of which all men and angels are good is justice, evil in rational creatures can be nothing but injustice (Ca 9). When the will of Satan abandoned the uprightness in which he was created there was nothing but a great absence or privation left for him, and that is the evil into which he fell.

Inseparable in its turn from this concept of evil and sin in the rational soul as consisting in the absence of justice or righteousness is the Anselmian emphasis on 'ought' and 'fittingness'. The righteousness which comes from God and which is bestowed on the will confers on that will an obligation to will in accordance with justice. The obligation remains even when the will voluntarily abandons justice (Ca 16; cf. 10–12). This is essential to Anselm's argument, for otherwise justice or its absence would be a matter of indifference from the point of view of blame, for one cannot be blamed for nothing. When once justice or righteousness has been given, says Anselm, the absence of justice must be called injustice, and that injustice becomes blameworthy, for the will has lost what it ought to have, and that 'ought' is indeed a something (Ca 16).

Anselm uses a similar device for explaining how nothing may be something in his account of the way in which God may be said to cause evil wills and evil actions. In so far as they are wills and actions they are 'something'. But the abandonment of the justice which ought to be present is caused by the creature's will, and so in so far as they are unjust actions or unjust wills, they are of the creature's making (Ca 20). Again, 'nothing' becomes 'something' in causing the consequences of evil. Injustice, like blindness, is nothing. But from it follow many disadvantages (*incommoditates*): injustice may cause a robbery; blindness may cause a man to fall into a pit. This is a principle well understood in such a sentence as 'The absence of a bridle causes the horse to bolt'. 'Ought' and 'fittingness' are in evidence again here; unfitting consequences come from the failure to do or to be as one ought (Ca 26).

In the *De Concordia* Anselm sets out a profoundly Augustinian view of the relationship between divine knowledge and created things. He poses the classic dilemma about God's authorship of evil. If God knows things which already exist, then they cannot be said to derive their existence from God. If things exist only because he knows them, then he must be said to be the creator of evil as well as good things. Anselm's solution is to say that everything which has existence must derive its being from God, and that includes all actions his creatures can do by acts of their own will. Such actions are in themselves good. But the wrong will of a creature in doing them can deprive them of their good, and then they become evil actions. The evil is simply the resulting absence of good in the thing which God has made good (C I.7).

So nothing is just or unjust, right or wrong in itself except justice and injustice. Everything that is, is of God's making, and therefore good (Co 4). Evil, which is identical with sin or unrighteousness, is itself nothing (Co 5). Just as blindness is the absence of sight where sight ought to be, so injustice is the absence of justice where justice ought to be (Co 5). But that does not mean that when God punishes for sin he punishes for nothing. He does not punish for their injustice those creatures which have no obligation to be just, that is beasts without rational wills. He simply exacts from men and women the honour due to him which they have been unwilling to pay and sets them apart from the just in a way which preserves the 'right order' of the universe (Co 6).

These are the presuppositions Anselm brings to the question 'Why did God become man?' They govern the way he understands the problem and the direction in which he looks for a solution. They are of the first importance in focusing his mind, and if they are also limiting, Anselm is well able to make a virtue out of that limitation in what is his most ambitious and challenging book.

Anselm's case in the *Cur Deus Homo* turns upon a strong doctrine of the seriousness of sin. It is serious to go against the will of God, in however trifling a matter. He takes an example. Suppose someone were in the presence of God, and was told to look in a certain direction by a bystander. God says that it is against his will for that glance to be taken. In itself the matter is tiny, a mere turning of the eyes. But what, asks Anselm, among all that exists, is important enough to be worth going against God's will? Even if one were faced with the alternative of doing a small thing against God's will or seeing the whole created world perish, the loss of the world would not be worth weighing in the balance against the absolute imperative of doing God's will (CDH I.21).

Note

1   See G. R. Evans, *Augustine on Evil* (Cambridge, 1983).

7

Why God became man

I

Anselm gave his own account of the writing of the *Cur Deus Homo* in its preface. He began it in England, where he made what progress with it he could in the early days of his archbishopric, and finished it in what he himself felt to be an unsatisfactory hurry in exile in Capua. Some of those who had access to his papers were so anxious to ensure that the work was published that they began making copies of the earlier parts before it was completed and polished, and Anselm says that for that reason he felt it necessary to publish the whole as soon as he could, so that there might be no confusion. One result has been that the work is shorter than he would have wished. He had wanted to develop a number of things he has left unsaid. It is hard to say whether in thus hurrying him the copyists saved a work which might have been lost or did a disservice in depriving us of matter which might have been there in a longer book; Anselm had a good record for finishing things in the end, and on balance it seems likely that their interference was for the worse.

Anselm explains that his method has been to set aside for purposes of argument all that we know of Christ by revelation through Scripture and to seek to demonstrate *remoto Christo*, without starting from the fact of Christ, whether we need to postulate that fact of Christ in order to make sense of events. He has chosen this means of demonstrating the absolute necessity of God's becoming man in order to meet the objections of 'unbelievers' (perhaps principally the Jews to whom Anselm's former pupil Gilbert Crispin, now abbot of

Westminster, had recently addressed his *Disputation between a Jew and a Christian*).[1] He has, in other words, chosen the hardest route so as to gain the proof which will convince the largest number of people. The two books into which Anselm divided the work have different purposes, he says. The first seeks to show that no one can possibly be saved without the work of Christ in becoming man and dying on the Cross; the second that human nature was created so that the whole man, body and soul, should be happy for eternity and that this end could be attained only by means of this same 'becoming man' on God's part. Here—in an echo of his promise at the beginning of the *Proslogion*—he assures the reader that he will show that all the things we believe about Christ must necessarily be so (Preface).

It is my habit, says Anselm, to answer those who ask me questions by showing them the reasonableness of the point of faith in question (CDH I.1). He finds that the method of question and answer is helpful to many people, particularly those who do not find abstract reasoning easy to follow, so he has taken as a partner in dialogue Boso, one of his own monks, who has been particularly energetic with questions on this subject. Boso takes the part of the 'unbeliever', at least in principle, though as the two become more and more engrossed in the discussion he slips out of his role from time to time. As he himself says, commenting on experience of such discussions in the past, it often happens that something becomes clear as one goes on that was not apparent at first (CDH I.1) and we see him as well as Anselm in pursuit of such illuminations as 'God discloses' to them in the course of the argument (CDH I.1). This is, then, different in character from Anselm's earlier 'educational' dialogues. Here is no 'pupil', led by his master from point to point, with the master keeping the end in view and controlling not only the outcome, but the technical details which need to be brought in for the pupil to master on the way. This is the record, turned into a literary and theological unity and ultimately of course taken into Anselm's own hands, of a real common inquiry, in which Anselm has learned from the discussion as well as Boso and the other friends and enquirers he represents.

Anselm has two substantial reservations at the outset, which he allows Boso to overcome for him. He says that there is such beauty and mystery in their subject that he fears he will not be able to do it justice either in thought or in the beauty of expression which writing about it seems to require. He himself is often indignant when he sees a badly painted picture of Christ. If his verbal picture is badly painted it will deserve just such contempt (CDH I.1). This is an important comment, because it shows how conscious and deliberate was Anselm's practice of adapting his style to his purpose and how much art there is in his writing. Boso reassures him that he will not be writing for those who will put style above all else, 'but for me and for those who are seeking an answer with me', that is, for the sincere enquirer (CDH I.1).

The second objection is philosophical. He cannot see how to treat this subject adequately without first writing at length on the subjects of 'will, power and necessity'. These seem to him, with some other notions, to be so interrelated that it is impossible to examine them separately. Boso suggests that it may prove to be possible to speak briefly about those aspects of these topics which are relevant to the discussion as it proceeds, and to save to another work a full discussion of the whole complex of problems. [2] There may be another echo here, this time of what Anselm did in treating of truth in the *Monologion*, where he took the subject up later and wrote a book about it in its own right (CDH I.1).

II

The particular objections of the unbelievers to whom Anselm is addressing himself concern the apparent indignity of God's descending into a woman's womb and being born and suckled, and growing up to be a man subject to weariness, hunger, thirst, and so on (CDH I.3). Anselm's first argument in response is to point out that the greater and more surprising the action the greater the degree of love and graciousness towards mankind which is revealed by the action. Secondly, he points to the appropriateness of putting right an act of disobedience on the part of fallen man by an act of supreme obedience. Many parallels can be drawn (the role of the tree in the Fall, the role of the Tree in the crucifixion, for example) which reinforce our sense of the beauty and fittingness of what was done (CDH I.3). But Anselm knows that these arguments and others like them seem to unbelievers to be no more than pictures. They are not convinced by them (CDH I.4). We must look for more hard-edged arguments.

Anselm starts from the premises that it was not fitting that God's plan for his precious work, the human race, should be thwarted. He assumes an agreed platform of assumption about the omnipotence and omniscience of God in saying this, for the point turns on the absolute requirement that what God intends shall come to pass (CDH I.4).

It seems on the face of it that if mankind had to be rescued it would have been more appropriate for God to depute some human being or angel for the task rather than humble himself (CDH I.5). Surely God could have created another man who was without sin, an entirely fresh creation, who could have done what was necessary? But there is a substantial objection to that idea. Such a man would have earned the service of those he rescued. Mankind was created to serve God alone, and to be the equal of angels (CDH I.5). The same objection would prevent the use of an angel to do the necessary work. Only God, it seems, could rescue man without creating such an anomaly.

That established, Anselm turns to examine the notion of 'redemption'. What sort of imprisonment was involved? In what captivity was the human race held that God could free it only by so much effort? Anselm describes the enslavement of sin, the just anger of God and the power of the Devil over those who are sinners. The 'unbelievers' ask why God could not simply exert his omnipotence to free men and women from slavery to sin, forget his own anger and bring the Devil, who cannot stand up to the Almighty, to heel? Although we may concede that only God could save mankind, they say, we do not at all see why it had to be done in the way you say it was (CDH I.6).

Anselm tackles first a question which we know to have been current in contemporary[3] academic debate, because it crops up in the records of the work of schools in northern France at this date: whether the Devil had any actual rights over man. If he did, then part of what needed to be done was the payment of a ransom to the Devil to deliver mankind. Anselm has no quarrel with the feudal imagery in which this position is expressed. But he cannot accept that the Devil can have any rights in the matter. Those who have submitted themselves to him as sinners he has stolen from God their rightful Lord. It cannot be necessary to pay a ransom to a usurper and a thief. Thus Anselm puts the Devil out of the picture at the outset (CDH I.7). The inclusion of this passage is of interest because it shows that the 'unbelievers', if they were indeed principally Jews, were in some measure acquainted[4] with contemporary Christian theological speculation, even, in a loose sense, part of the academic community, if we may call it that.

In answer to the objection that it cannot be proper to impute to God a humility wholly alien to the Supreme Being, Anselm answers that what Christians believe is in no way inimical to the belief that the divine nature cannot change or suffer. When God became man, God was not diminished; instead, man was exalted. Nothing we affirm of Christ as regards the weakness of his human nature is to be attributed to his divine nature. The two remain distinct in his incarnate Person.

There remains the question of the willingness of Christ to suffer. The 'unbelievers' argue that it cannot have been reasonable or just in God to deliver up to death his own Son whom he loved, and who was when he became man, the most just of all men (CDH I.8). If God could not save sinners in any other way than by condemning a just man, where is his omnipotence? If he could have done it in another way and chose not to, where is his wisdom and his justice? All these difficulties disappear, says Anselm, if we realize that the Son was not forced. Here the complex of will, power and necessity resolves itself easily. The Son willed to die. But, argues Boso on behalf of the unbelievers, Scripture contains a number of passages which seem to suggest that there was some submission of will to the Father as though under constraint. He 'humbled himself and became obedient to the Father unto death' (Philippians 2:8–9) he 'learned obedience by the things he suffered' (Hebrews 5:8); 'the Father . . . delivered him up for us all' (Romans 8:32). We need to distinguish here, says Anselm, between active obedience to command and that which occurs as a result of a habit of living in a right relation to God. Every rational creature ought as a fundamental obligation of its nature to hold steadily to justice and truth in deed and word. When he became man, the Son owed that obedience to God. When he was persecuted and crucified, it was a result of his persevering in this obedience which is simply living rightly. No compulsion to die can have come from God in this. God created all rational beings to be happy in the enjoyment of God, and he would never make such a creature unhappy through no fault of its own. To meet death against one's will is unhappiness. So God cannot have compelled Christ to do that. We must conclude that Christ willingly underwent death, not obeying any command to give up his life, but going steadily on in justice and willingly taking the consequences (CDH I.9).

III

We come now to the question of satisfaction for sin. Anselm offers three principles as a starting-point. Man was created for happiness, which cannot be possessed in this life. No one can attain happiness unless his sins have been forgiven. No one lives out his life without sin. It follows that before man can attain happiness, his sins must be forgiven (CDH I.9). Sinning is defined as not rendering to God what one ought. What ought to be thus rendered is obedience to the will of God. (Anselm has at his disposal in Latin a word—*debere*—which carries both the sense of 'owe' and the sense of 'ought', so that he is able to see this obligation in terms of a debt to God.) Uprightness of heart which perseveres in giving up the will to God pays him the honour which is due to him, and not to do so dishonours God. (Here Anselm is unconsciously adopting a feudal frame of reference, in which the notion of the honour due to a lord is mixed in with the Biblical concept of God as Lord.) Making up for such dishonouring involves not only paying what was originally owed, that is, conforming one's will to that of God, but also something more, a restoring of honour where there has been insult. Satisfaction for sin must include both elements (CDH I.11).

Boso thinks it reasonable to ask whether God can forgive sin out of mercy alone and not require the satisfaction due. Anselm's reply is that that would leave a disorder unresolved, which would be *inconveniens*, disharmonious, out of keeping with the divine nature (CDH I.12). Does the punishment of a sinner, then, do God honour (CDH I.14)? Yes, says Anselm, because it restores the balance of mastery and a kind of symmetry. (For by sinning a man seizes what belongs to God, and by punishing him God overrides his will and thus takes from him that freedom of choice which is his: I.14.)

But by the same argument, says Boso, surely it ought to be impossible for God's honour to be violated in the first place? That brings about the disorder which Anselm has just maintained to be impossible with God. Certainly, Anselm answers, God's honour cannot be added to or subtracted from in itself. When a rational nature does what it ought to do it does not add anything to God's honour, and in the same way, when it fails in obedience it takes nothing away. The disorder occurs in the created realm, where change and decay are possible, and put right there, where God's will is that order shall ultimately be maintained (CDH I.15).

Anselm now permits himself a digression on the subject of angels. He had long ago shown an interest in them in choosing to write in the

De Casu Diaboli on the fall of Satan rather than the fall of man as the focus of his inquiry into the way free choice can go wrong. Here he postulates that God intended to make up from human nature the due and ordained number of inhabitants of the heavenly city, so that his original plan for it should not be frustrated. Boso concedes that that is what he believes (and here he has forgotten his role of advocate for the 'unbelievers'). But he would like a reason for it. The passage is illuminating for Anselm's methodology and assumptions, and is worth pausing over for a moment here. He begins from the idea that there must exist a perfect number of inhabitants of the heavenly city. There are two possibilities. Either God created additional angels knowing that some would fall, which would mean that they fell of necessity; or he created the perfect number or a number within that total, also foreseeing that some would fall, and making provision for making up the perfect number in his plan to create mankind. The first alternative can be dismissed, because it would make God the author of the angels' fall. We must discount the possibility that the number was to be left imperfect after the fall of the angels, for that would frustrate God's intention and leave an everlasting disorder in heaven (CDH I.16). God could not make fresh angels to replace those who had fallen because that would create inequality in heaven. The first creation of angels would have the merit of having persevered purely out of obedience; any second creation would know the consequences of disobedience and their obedience would be of a different order. Anselm refers the reader to his *De Casu Diaboli* for a discussion of the idea of perseverance and its relevance here (CDH I.17). There is a subsidiary but attractive question (and one discussed in contemporary schoolrooms, at the cathedral school of Laon, as perhaps Anselm knew) as to whether the number of the elect among men was simply to equal that of the fallen angels, which would imply that man had been created solely in order to make up numbers in heaven, or whether the number of men in heaven was to be greater than that of the fallen angels. That would imply that God had always intended to create mankind and had made space for them in his plan for the heavenly city. Anselm prefers that view, and says that even if no angel had perished, human beings would have had a place of their own in the heavenly city. He finds in all this an argument for the view that whether or not men were created later than angels, there was flexibility in the pattern of things which would allow the angels freely to choose to persevere or not to persevere. It must, he feels, be the case that men were to be created anyway, since otherwise the elect among men would have reason to rejoice over the fall of the angels as having provided room for them, and that cannot be consonant with righteousness (CDH I.18).

This apparent digression proves to be very much to the point. If it was always part of God's plan to replace from among men those angels whom he foresaw would fall, he must also have intended that these were to be the equals of the angels who persevered. To let off the sinners among men without exacting satisfaction would be to create inequality in heaven; or, rather, it would be to put a sinner on a par with a good angel. Anselm illustrates the point with a picture. Suppose a rich man had in his hand a pearl of great price which he is about to place in his treasury. Suppose he permits someone to knock it from his hand into the mud. Would he pick it up and put it straight into his treasury without cleaning it? Man's equality with his fellow-citizens of heaven depends upon his being made really sinless, really restored to what he was before (CDH I.19).

To make satisfaction is not merely to pay what is owed, but to do something more, argues Anselm (CDH I.21). There is an injury to be mended as well as a failure which needs to be made good. When Adam allowed himself to be vanquished by Satan he took something away from God (CDH I.23), that is, his intention for the human race. It is necessary not only that that intention now be carried out, but also that man who took it away should restore what was God's. That is to say, man himself must make the reparation. Supreme justice could accept nothing less (CDH I.23).

If man cannot pay to God the debt he owes, ought he not in some sense to be excused? That might be so, argues Anselm, if he were unable to pay through no fault of his own. But that is not the case. Suppose a master tells his servant to carry out a certain task, and at the same time instructs him not to throw himself into a deep hole from which he will not be able to get out. If the servant takes no notice and voluntarily leaps into the hole, is he not to be blamed because he cannot now carry out the task he was given (CDH I.24)? That is the situation in which mankind has placed itself. Unrighteousness is therefore twofold: the failure to do what one ought and culpability for that failure.

IV

With the beginning of the second book of the *Cur Deus Homo* Anselm turns to the positive side of the dark story of man's hopeless debt. God created man to be happy in the enjoyment of his presence.

If he had not sinned man would not have died (CDH II.1–2), for it is inconceivable that God would have placed the barrier of death between his first loving and desiring the highest Good and his eternal enjoyment of that Good. After death, in the restored community, human beings will have again the bodies in which they lived, for only in that way can the restoration of God's original purpose be perfect. God will thus accomplish in human nature the purpose he first had for mankind (CDH II.3–4). These are the fundamentals.

We now come to the question of necessity. Anselm has rested a good deal on ideas about the importance of God's purpose being fulfilled. But does that not amount to a constraint upon God? The very 'necessity' of avoiding *inconvenientia* in his actions would seem on the face of it to place limitations on what God can do. Here Anselm makes much the same distinction as he used in the case of Christ's willingness to die. If someone enters monastic life, he makes a vow which he is thereafter under a necessity to keep. But if he does so willingly, no constraint is involved. He lives as he is obliged to live, but in absolute freedom. God, who knew all that would ensue, freely bound himself to the rules of the necessity which would govern the process of man's salvation when he created Adam. This voluntary placing of himself in a position where he must save mankind as he did is an act of supreme generosity, and it compels our gratitude to an infinitely greater degree than a slavish doing what is necessary could ever do (CDH II.6).

Anselm now comes to the nub of the whole treatise. Drawing together the threads of all that he has said, he argues that the salvation of mankind can only be accomplished if someone pays to God something which is sufficient to make recompense, and that must be something which is greater than every existing thing other than God. The person who can make this payment must himself be greater than everything which is not God. Only God himself fulfils this requirement (an echo of the *Proslogion*'s definition of God here). So only God himself can make this satisfaction. But only a man ought to make it; that is to say, the debt is man's. For God to pay it would not be for man to make satisfaction. So it seems that it is necessary for a being who is both God and man (*deus homo*) to make the satisfaction which is necessary. Boso exclaims, 'Blessed be God!' at this juncture, to mark the importance of what they have discovered (CDH II.6).

But this is a stupendous concept. How can such a being exist? The divine nature and the human nature cannot be changed into one another. Nor is it possible that they can fuse to form a third nature which is neither fully divine nor fully human (for that would not fulfil the necessary conditions). On the other hand, if they are not in some manner truly joined, the necessary conditions will still not be fulfilled, for the divine will not be obliged to make satisfaction and the human will not be able to. Anselm's theology of satisfaction carries within it a theology of incarnation which demonstrates the necessity of the union of two natures in one Person (CDH II.7).

Anselm moves now to the task of working out the details of the mode of incarnation necessary to fulfil the required conditions. God could simply have made a new man. But such a man would not belong to the race born of Adam, and so he would not owe the debt. If, then, the Man who was to redeem the world had to be born of Adam's stock, there seem to be three possibilities. For him to be born of a man and a woman seems to Anselm less 'pure' and less 'honourable' than for him to be born of one alone. God had already shown that it was possible for him to make another of Adam's race from a man alone, in creating Eve. Now he demonstrated that it was possible for him to make a man from a woman alone. It does not seem to Anselm worth asking whether this was more fittingly to be done from a virgin or not. Besides, it has the symmetry of repairing the damage originally done to the human race by the virgin Eve (CDH II.8).

To this new man God joined not all three Persons of the Trinity but only one, for as we have seen, the only way in which the divine and human natures of the God-Man could be conjoined was in a single Person (II.9). Anselm repeats very briefly here the arguments he had advanced in the *De Incarnatione* (to which he refers the reader) to show that it was necessary that it was the Son and not the Holy Spirit or the Father who was incarnate (II.9).

But surely if this new man was sinless (because he was God) there was no reason why he should be mortal? We have already established that Adam would not have died if he had not sinned. And if the God-Man did not die, he could not have saved mankind. Anselm feels it useful to go back rather further and look into the implications of the not-sinning of both Christ and the good angels, who also now cannot sin. He needs to show that it is praiseworthy not to sin, even where sin is impossible. We are brought back again here to the territory of one of Anselm's earlier treatises and the topic of freedom of choice. It seems that Christ was both able to sin and not able to sin. For example, he says (John 8:55), 'If I say that I do not know him, I shall be a liar like you'. Now he could certainly utter the words, 'I do not know him', so it was possible for him to be a liar, and thus to sin. But we must understand 'if he willed it', and recognize that it was impossible for him so to will because he would never freely choose to do so. So his not-sinning was a matter of free choice not of inability of a sort which implies weakness or constraint. Similarly, in a lesser sense, the good angels who now cannot sin have this ability not to sin from themselves (CDH II.10) So the sinless Christ and, *mutatis mutandis*, the good angels who cannot sin are both unable to sin and deserving of praise because they do not sin. Why then did God not create men and angels from the first in that condition? Because then they would have been like Christ himself, very God, says Anselm. We have established, then, that Christ could not be required to die because he was not a sinner (CDH II.10).

How, then, was he able to die? Anselm makes a case for the view that mortality pertains not to human nature in itself, that is, not to human nature when it is without sin as it was created to be, but to human nature corrupted by sin. It was therefore possible for Christ to be a real man and still not mortal. But he was also God, and in his omnipotence able to will to lay down his life and take it up again. Equally he can will to be able to be killed if he so chooses. We can say with confidence that his death was under no compulsion, either such as would weigh against his omnipotence, or such as would follow from his being a sinner; he died of his own free will (CDH II.11).

This opens up the question how far, as a man, Christ was able to share human infirmities. Anselm holds that whatever he suffered as a man was not able to shadow his tranquillity as God, for he suffered willingly, accepting a pain which thus became no pain at all to him (CDH II.12). Moreover, he never shared our ignorance, for from the first moment of incarnate life he was in full possession of his divine power, might and wisdom (CDH II.13) This line of argument is wholly in keeping with Anselm's doctrine that as man, Christ lifted up human nature rather than diminishing his divinity to come down to human level; it is also an endorsement of the principles of Augustinian Platonism which remained foundational to all his thought.

V

We come now to the question of the way in which this death can be said to count against sin, especially against all the mass of sin perpetrated by rational natures. If one small sin is so important that it would be worth losing the world to avoid it, how can all sin together be outweighed? Anselm demonstrates that the life of Christ was of more value than all sin together is detestable. So if his life were given for sin, it would wipe it out in its entirety. And it was so given, when he willingly accepted death (CDH II.14). It blots out even the sin of those who put him to death (CDH II.15). And it is so great a gift that it deserves a reward. But the Son already has all that the Father has to give. So it is entirely reasonable that the Father should give the reward to those for whom the Son wanted it, that is, for mankind (CDH II.20)

As in most of his writings, Anselm set out in the *Cur Deus Homo* to answer a specific question. He did not attempt a treatise covering the whole conspectus of issues about Christology and redemption which were familiar to him from his reading. Even in the generation after him, other aspects were attracting interest. In his commentary on Romans, Peter Abelard dismisses Anselm's account of the reason why God became man, along with others, and proposes the view that his prime purpose was to set an example of the way a human life should be lived. We find such reflections in Anselm only within the framework of the prayers and meditations. We must look there, too, for any treatment of the experience of suffering as something Christ chose to share with man, or of the notion of a sacrifice made not only on our behalf but in fellowship and common experience with us. The prayers focused on Christ and the Cross and those addressed to Mary must be set beside the Meditation on Human Redemption here. Anselm's understanding of why God became man embraces all that is said there, and these devotional writings round out the sometimes seemingly rather mechanistic explanations of fine theological points in the *Cur Deus Homo*. They also set the *Cur Deus Homo* in a context which makes it altogether more modern because they show how deeply central Anselm's theories of 'right' and 'honour' and 'obligation' and 'order' are to his awareness of the muddle and confusion and pain of ordinary human experience.

Notes

1   Gilbert Crispin's *Disputatio cum Judaeo* and the *Disputatio cum Gentili* are edited by A. Abulafia and G. R. Evans, *The Works of Gilbert Crispin* (London, 1986).

2   This other work, in embryo, may be the Philosophical Fragments.

3   See O. Lottin, *Psychologie et morale aux xiie et xiiie siècles*, V (Gembloux, 1959).

4   B. Smalley, *The Study of the Bible in the Middle Ages* (3rd edn, Oxford, 1983).

8

'A most famous question'

I

In the *De Conceptu Virginali* Anselm pursues one of the questions
which had arisen while he was writing the *Cur Deus Homo*. How was
it possible for God to assume a sinless human nature when the whole
human race was in slavery to original sin? He begins by seeking a
definition of original sin, for it is here that the difficulty lies. The
word 'original' must refer either to the origin of human nature itself,
or to the origin of sin in each individual. The first cannot give us the
meaning of 'original sin', since Adam and Eve were created without
sin. We must look in the second place, in the origin of each human
person for the source of original sin in him. Anselm does not see any
necessity to choose between a traducianist and a creationist view
here, any more than Augustine did. It does not matter whether the
human soul is somehow handed down genetically as is the human
body, or freshly created for each new human being (Co 1).

Anselm holds that in each human being a nature and a person are
present. The nature makes him human, being a 'person'
distinguishes him from other members of the human race (Co 1).
There is sin in both, in human nature, that sin which is called
'original'; and in the person, the actual sins committed by that
individual (Co 1). The personal sin of Adam and Eve corrupted their
natures so pervasively that all their progeny inherited the corruption
with their very humanity. But there remained in that corrupt human
nature two obligations: to possess and maintain the perfect justice
God had given; and to make satisfaction for having abandoned it.
These obligations too all men and women inherit in their nature
(Co 3).

The whole human race existed in Adam 'causally' or 'materially' because they were there as seed. But when an infant is born it exists as an individual person. So we may distinguish sin deriving from a nature and sin deriving from a person (Co 23). But the sin in the nature infects the person, and in time all human persons commit sins as a result (Co 23).

Because of the implication that miscarried foetuses would be condemned to an eternity of punishment, Anselm suggests that original sin cannot be present in the infant from the moment of conception. Original sin is injustice, a lack of that uprightness which ought to be there, and uprightness is lodged in the will of rational creatures. Only when the unborn child is sufficiently mature to be said to be a rational being can original sin be present, and then it will inescapably be there as a fact of his corrupted human nature (Co 3–7). How, then, can man be said to be conceived in sin? It is an accepted usage (also found in Scripture), Anselm suggests, to say of something whose futurity is certain that it is in fact the case (Co 7). So the sin is not in the seed from which the infant is conceived, but there is in the seed the inevitability that when the foetus reaches a point where the infant has a rational soul, he will also have original sin.

This gives Anselm the principle he needs from which to demonstrate how it was possible for Christ to be born of the Virgin and to be fully human, without being tainted with original sin. The original sin in which infants are born amounts to nothing more than an inability to make satisfaction, to do what they ought as God's rational creatures. In the case of Christ we must show that this did not apply (Co 8).

He suggests that it is helpful to begin by separating three ways in which things come about. Some things occur by God's power and will alone. Some come to pass through created nature in its ordinary course. Some happen by the will of creatures (Co 11). The birth of Christ from a Virgin fell into neither the second nor the third category, but the first; it was a miracle. So we may postulate certain distinctive features of his birth (Co 11). Chief among them is his freedom from the helplessness of other men and women in the matter of right willing and making satisfaction. Indeed, it would not be right for him to have been helpless in this way (Co 12).

If I call a man blind I mean that he lacks sight in his eyes, where sight ought to be. I do not mean that the whole man is blind. Similarly, a deaf man is deaf only in his ears, where hearing

85

ought to be. To call the human race *en masse* 'sinful' is not to impute sinfulness to anything but the wills of men, where uprightness ought to be.

Now we have established that at the moment of conception the foetus does not have a will, and so there was no reason why Christ need have been tainted by original sin just because he was born from the 'mass' of the human race. His will was otherwise than that of ordinary men and women, and so the taint of sin never arose in him as it would in any other human infant as it matured (Co 15).

If it is to be argued that the child Jesus was free of sin because his birth was miraculous and he thus escaped the usual consequences of the development of will in the child, why, some ask, did that not also apply to the case of John the Baptist and others who were born miraculously (from sterile or elderly parents)? This was not the same, replies Anselm. In their case what happened lay within the natural order, although it required divine intervention to make it possible. John and others like him were born of parents in whom what was natural had been restored to function, and so they were born by means of the reproductive nature which was given to Adam (Co 16).

(It is also asked by some why, if God was able to make from Adam as many sinless beings as he needed to fill up the city of Heaven, it was necessary for him to become incarnate in the Son. Could God not have fulfilled his original intention in that way? That would not have wiped out the damage and dishonour done, says Anselm, and in any case, that would have made the gift of the power to reproduce themselves useless to Adam and Eve, for God would be sidestepping the reproductive method natural to humanity. That would have implied that his original creation was imperfect: Co 17.)

This centrality of will as making a human being both a person and (as things stand since Adam) a sinner, was explored by Anselm in a series of treatises.

II

Anselm left a subject unfinished and returned to it later only twice: in writing the *Proslogion* when he had completed the *Monologion*, and in writing on the relationship between divine will, power and necessity, and human will. The 'most famous question' of the way in which human freedom of choice can be possible in the face of divine grace, foreknowledge and predestination was well known to him through his reading of Augustine, and he may have had some knowledge of the Carolingian debates in which Godescalc d'Orbais had been at the centre of a row about whether a God who predestines the elect for heaven must not in some sense also predestine the remainder of mankind for hell and thus be himself the author of their evil. His own work in this area began with the treatise *On Freedom of Choice* (*De Libertate Arbitrii*), which forms part of the series of little treatises for beginners in the study of Scripture. He went on to ask how it can have been possible for the angels to sin (*De Casu Diaboli*). Much later, among the last of his treatises, he attempted in the *De Concordia* a 'harmony' of free will, grace, predestination and divine foreknowledge.

It is of some significance that he chose to concentrate in the *De Libertate Arbitrii* not on the nature of the will, as Augustine had done in his differently titled *De Libero Arbitrio*, but on the nature of the freedom of choice it exercises. Thus in the 'three little treatises' he concentrates on truth, freedom and evil primarily as concepts and as realities in themselves, and only secondarily as they affect human and angelic lives.

The problem presents itself first in the *De Libertate Arbitrii* as one of seeming opposition between forces which make absolute demands. This is the classic difficulty. It may be put in various ways. If, for example, God is omniscient and omnipotent, how can any creature really have freedom to change his mind and choose another course of action, since his future is foreseen and God cannot be wrong? Anselm puts it another way. If we always have freedom of choice, why do we need grace? And if we do not always have freedom of choice, why is sin imputed to us, since we sin without being able to help it? (L 1). Augustine taught that one of the effects of the Fall has been utterly to destroy the capacity of the human will ever to choose good without God's help, while leaving it 'free' to choose evil of itself. We have seen hints of Anselm's accepting this view in the prayers and meditations in his descriptions of the helplessness of his own will to do good. But here he robustly alters the terms of the discussion in order to avoid the traditional impasse between human and divine freedom, and specifically to resolve the contradiction he has stated. The solution must lie in the definition of 'freedom of choice', he suggests.

Anselm argues that freedom of choice is not 'the capacity to sin or not to sin' it is frequently assumed to be. Augustine's notion of a maimed will which has lost its access to one of two options is wrong, not in its picture of the effects of sin in fallen man, but in its conception of the original freedom of choice which Adam lost. If freedom of choice allowed one to choose both good and evil, neither God nor the good angels would have freedom of choice (L 1). Freedom of choice must simply be the ability not to sin. The capacity to sin would decrease the will's freedom; when it is taken away it increases the will's freedom. So it can itself be neither freedom nor a part of freedom (*ibid.*).

This stepping behind the familiar framework of the problem is the starting-point for a radically new account of the matter. Anselm goes on to define all freedom as ability (L 3), and to distinguish in a way which foreshadows the later mediaeval use made of Aristotle's distinction between *potestas* and *actus*,[1] between ability and the concomitant circumstances which make ability usable. No ability taken by itself, he points out, would be 'able' to do anything. Anyone who can see, can see a mountain, but if there is no mountain to see, or it is dark, he would have to admit that he could see no mountain. Nevertheless, the capacity to see a mountain remains in him undiminished. In exactly this way, Anselm contends, the capacity to maintain rightness of will is always there in rational natures. It is simply that, in fallen man, the concomitant conditions without which it cannot be used are missing (L 3, 4).

Anselm enlarges upon the principle that the capacity to choose good is itself freedom of choice. This definition he argues, resolves at a stroke the difficulty about an apparent conflict between human freedom of choice and divine freedom of choice. Indeed we may say that although God can turn everything he made back into the nothing from which he made it, he cannot take away rightness of willing from human good will. In choosing the good the free will automatically wills what God wants it to will. Were God to will to take away that rightness of willing, the good human will would will that too. But for God to do so would be for him to create a contradiction, for the good will would be obliged to go along with his will that it should no longer will what he wants (L 8). The definition also underlines the utter freedom of a 'freedom of choice' which is simply the capacity to choose the good; for nothing outside itself can ever take away that freedom if God himself cannot do so (L 9).

The reverse is the case in the slavery of our subjection to sin. That we cannot alter by our own ability. We can be drawn away from servitude to sin only by someone else (L 11). Here the pupil raises a difficulty. How can I be both a slave and free? Anselm explains that we should not think of servitude to sin as opposed to freedom of choice (in the Augustinian way). The freedom to keep uprightness of will, we have agreed, is an ability or capacity, and that remains in all circumstances, although it can only be acted upon in certain conditions. The servitude to sin from which we cannot rescue ourselves is in opposition strictly speaking to an uprightness of will from which only we ourselves can separate us. The underlying freedom remains in both (L 11).

Anselm ends with a summary of the principles he has been establishing. In God there is a freedom of choice which is unique to him and which has no origin because it is neither created nor received. In men and angels there is a created freedom of choice. In both there was at first a distinction between the created freedom of choice which has uprightness in such a way that it cannot lose it, and that which has uprightness in such a way that it is able to lose it. The first is found in the good angels and in men and women who are among the elect, but in the angels only since the fall of the wicked angels and in the elect among people only after their death. The second was found in all angels before the fall of the wicked ones and the confirmation of the good; and in those men and women who keep uprightness of will during their lives. There is also a created freedom which has no uprightness to maintain. This is found both in those human beings who never regain their uprightness and, in a different form, in the fallen angels, for it is impossible that they should ever regain their uprightness. In all these distinctions, Anselm consistently maintains the presence of freedom. Even the reprobate angels have a created freedom, although they have no uprightness and are condemned to remain without it for eternity.

In the *De Casu Diaboli* Anselm pursues these ramifications in an attempt to show how it was possible for angelic beings to sin. Our immediate concern here is with the topics of the *De Concordia*. Anselm tackles there, as distinct questions, the problems of the apparent incompatibility of freedom of choice with, first, divine foreknowledge, second, predestination and third, the grace of God.

III

Foreknowledge and freedom of choice
The difficulty here concerns the nature of futurity. Anselm was familiar with the discussion in Aristotle's *De Interpretatione*

through the medium of Boethius, for whom this was a question of special interest. The philosophical problem concerns the truth of statements in the future tense. If I say, 'There will be a sea-fight tomorrow', my statement can only be true when I make it if the future is determined. If futurity is in any way contingent and not necessary, it would seem that no statement in the future tense can be true or false, but only statements in the present or the past tense.[2] Anselm poses a different problem, but one in which the distinction between contingent and necessary futurity proves to be important. He presents his problem like this: What God foresees has a necessary futurity, for it is impossible that he should be wrong about the future. What is freely chosen will happen without any necessity. It seems on the face of it that nothing can have both a necessary and a contingent futurity, so that God's foreknowledge cannot coexist with human freedom of choice about future actions.

Anselm proceeds by positing both divine foreknowledge and human freedom of choice so as to see whether it is indeed impossible for the two to coexist. In so doing, he is recognizing the imperative claims of both to exist within the framework of Christian orthodoxy and seeking to show that they are compatible to reason too.

Anselm suggests that necessary futurity may be seen as in some sense containing contingent futurity. God foresees even those things which are going to occur without necessity, since he foreknows all future events. It becomes, paradoxically, necessary for something to occur without necessity. The pupil, subsumed here in a series of imagined objections and comments ('But you will say to me. . . . Perhaps you will claim'), objects that that seems to imply coercion of the will. If what I am to choose is known to God and is therefore necessary, surely I really have no choice (C I.1)? Anselm argues that necessity does not always imply coercion of the will. If we say 'It is necessary for God to be immortal' or 'It is necessary for God not to be unjust', we are not referring to any force compelling him to be immortal or prohibiting him from being unjust. Thus we may say, 'It is necessary that you are—or are not—going to sin of your own free will' and so include the voluntariness of the choice within the necessity of God's foreknowledge. No compulsion is involved. Similarly, there is no compulsion in God's foreknowing, for he can foreknow only what is in fact to happen. That is no more than to say that he can foreknow only the truth. 'If this will happen, it will happen of necessity' (C I.2). On these grounds we can accept the coexistence of my freedom of choice about my future actions and God's foreknowledge of them.

IV

Predestination and freedom of choice

But in the case of predestination it would seem that we are inescapably brought up against the problem of coercion. And a further difficulty arises, that if all that God foresees he also foreordains, he must be said to foreordain evil actions as well as good (C II.1). There is an important difference to be noted here, suggests Anselm, between the manner of speaking we use when we say (as Scripture does, Romans 9:18; Matthew 6:13), that God 'hardens' a man's heart, meaning that he does not soften it; or that he 'leads him into temptation' when we mean that he does not deliver him from temptation. In this way it can be said that God predestines evil men and evil actions when he does not correct the men or their actions (C II.2). But it would be a more 'proper' use of language to say that he foreknows and predestines good works, because there he is the cause both of the actions in themselves and the fact that they are good. Evil actions may be good in themselves, for all that exists is good (another Augustinian borrowing), but turned to evil by the will of man (C II.2).

Having dealt with the second of the new difficulties, Anselm returns to the first. We can be sure that God's foreknowledge and predestination do not conflict with one another, for there can be no inconsistency in God. But God cannot exercise coercion in the case of free acts of good will, for they would not then be good by the definition which makes justice the preservation of uprightness for its own sake. Though the will can do no good thing which God does not cause, God's causing is not a compulsion.

V

Grace and freedom of choice

Anselm says that God causes such good works not by coercion but by grace (C II.3). It is to the implications of this statement that he turns in the last section of the *De Concordia*. The problem here is that Scripture sometimes seems to speak as though grace alone and no element of freedom of choice brings us to salvation, and sometimes as though salvation were entirely dependent upon the exercise of freedom of choice. 'Without me you can do nothing' (John 15:5); 'What do you have that you have not received?' (1 Corinthians 4:7); but 'If you are willing and will listen to me, you shall eat the good

91

things of the land' (Isaiah 1:19); 'Turn away from evil and do good' (Psalm 33/34:13). Anselm knows that there are parties in the Church who argue, respectively, for 'grace alone' and for 'free will alone' (C III.1). Anselm sees both as essential for salvation, for those who have reached the age of reason (C III.2).[3] He places 'justice' at the heart of things. There is no doubt, if we look at Scripture, that those who are saved are saved because of justice. We have Anselm's definition that justice is the preservation of uprightness of will for its own sake. So right willing is necessary for salvation.

Anselm's doctrine of grace is close to Augustine's. But he adds a significant dimension with his theory of an uprightness which is grace's gift to human freedom of choice and which a man or woman freely 'receives' or refuses. To keep this uprightness once received is an act of will. But it is impossible to will it unless one possesses it. Thus grace preceding gives the uprightness, and a subsequent grace makes it possible to keep it. The 'keeping' of uprightness is therefore entirely at the disposal of grace at every point.

But the story is more complicated. Grace never denies this gift unless free choice abandons it by willing something else incompatible with it. So the loss of uprightness is the fault of the sinner alone.

And the uprightness must be unqualified for the sinner to be justified and to enjoy the happiness of heaven; it must be perfect justice or righteousness. This Anselm sees as involving right living. 'We know that a Christian can attain freedom from all unrighteousness by endeavouring to live a holy life by the grace of God' (C III.4).

Anselm moves now to a consideration of various Scriptural passages which show that the action of grace does not eliminate freedom of choice or freedom of choice exclude the need for grace. It is as though one were to give a naked man clothes. He may or may not choose to wear them, but if he does wear them the giver must be credited with the fact that he is clothed. God does more for the sinner naked in his sins. He also gives by grace the power to put on the clothes (C III.5). Particularly testing are the passages which seem to call people to good works and condemn them if they fail to do good works, in the light of the principle that they cannot do good at all without the help of grace. It seems on the face of it unjust to condemn the sinner for what it appears cannot be his fault. Here Anselm sets out more fully than anywhere else his doctrine of the Word of God in its working for salvation. If no one cultivates the earth it produces a multitude of plants, but many are noxious weeds and few are nourishing. Only the action of the farmer, in planting the right seeds and laboriously cultivating them, produces good food from the ground. Without learning and effort human hearts sprout plentiful thoughts and wishes, but they do not save, and are often inimical to salvation. The Word of God is the good seed, or, it would be more exact to say, Anselm suggests, the meaning of the Word is the good seed, for it is the meaning which acts upon the mind to make it produce good thoughts and right willing (C III.6). This meaning is itself a seed, for one cannot will what one does not know or have a conception of. Anselm quotes Romans 10:13–15 to illustrate the principle from Scripture. It is not, he argues, that the possession of the concept produces faith in the individual; rather, it should be regarded as a necessary condition of faith. When actual right willing follows the understanding of what it is to will rightly, grace produces faith, because the soul is believing what it hears.

This makes preaching of the first importance. The same passage from Romans asks, 'How shall they hear without a preacher, and how shall they preach unless they are sent?' The sending of preachers is, says Anselm, an act of divine grace. It follows that preaching itself is a grace, for what derives from grace is a grace; and by the same argument hearing is also a grace, and the understanding which results from hearing the preached Word is a grace, and the right willing which is a consequence of understanding is also a grace. All this is dependent on the soul's having first received the uprightness which makes all this growth possible.

VI

Anselm's doctrine of sanctification is, then, analogous with a picture of divine husbandry. Just as God in the beginning made wheat and other nourishing things to grow from the earth, so he made the Gospels and the hearts of prophets and apostles rich with seed of salvation. With the aid of God's husbandry of grace we receive the fruits of what we sow, for the nourishment of our souls. Anselm illustrates the process carefully from Scripture. Isaiah 45:22 has 'be converted to me'. This reminds us that the seed does not germinate until God bends a man or woman's will to will the conversion of which he or she has a conception as a result of hearing these words. In Luke 17:5 we read 'increase our faith'. These are the words of those who are already converted and who are asking for growth in holiness (C III.6).

The 'seed' analogy is helpful, too, in understanding the case of those who do not turn to God. God does not cause every seed to germinate, or foster its growth. But the 'farmers' who preach the Word do not for that reason fail to sow the seed. They sow in hope of even a small harvest. God commands that they do so, with serious intent and with hope. So it is never wrong or a waste of time to invite people to believe in Christ, even if they do not all accept the invitation (C III.7).

The happiness of which we are assured through faith and through baptism is not that which Adam and Eve had in paradise before they sinned. It is the happiness to which they were to come when the heavenly City was completed and its full numbers made up from angels and men. If those who are saved from sin were to be translated to happiness at once, says Anselm, heaven could not be filled, for in the heavenly City there will be no procreation of children, and so there would be no means of adding to the number of Adam's race. This is a further reason why it is under God's good providence that baptism does not transform us completely all at once (C III.9).

The whole process seems to Anselm analogous to what might happen to a servant whom his master had intended to heap with great honour, when that servant does his master a grievous wrong. The servant is scourged and beaten, and the master is about to thrust him into a dungeon when someone makes satisfaction for him and reconciles him with his master. The stripes (which were deserved) do not at once disappear; the servant must be healed of them gradually. But he is saved from the worse punishment which was about to come upon him, and because satisfaction has been complete, his master is able to give him the honour he originally intended for him. The honour is not affected by what has happened, because when he sinned and satisfaction was made for him, he did not yet have it, and so he could not be disinherited by his sin (C III.9).

What of those who try with all their might to live as they ought and repeatedly fail? It is often suggested, says Anselm, that this proves that free choice can do nothing. It is his own opinion that in such cases there is always some abandonment of truly upright willing, some willing of that which is incompatible with it (C III.10). This leads him to some reflections on the nature of the will. There seem to him to be three senses in which the word 'will' is used: to refer to the instrument which does the willing; to speak of the inclination itself; and to speak of the use of the will. The will as instrument is the power of the soul we use for willing, just as we use the reason as an instrument for reasoning and the sight as an instrument for seeing. The *affectio*, or inclination of the will, is a built-in tendency to will in certain directions and not others. (For example, the will would never will sickness.) The actual use of the will is confined to those occasions when we are conscious of using it (C III.11). Within this threefold structure are hidden two 'compound' wills: to want what is beneficial or profitable, a will inseparable from our having a will at all; and to will what is right, which can fail in us while leaving us still with something which can properly be called 'will'. Uprightness belongs to the will as instrument, and gives rise to a right inclination and right acts where it is present. This is the truth of the will which the Devil abandoned (John 8:44; cf. *De Veritate* 4). Human merit is wrapped up in the possession of this uprightness of will, just as was the merit of the angels (C III.12). God gave Adam all he needed to maintain that uprightness, as well as the power to abandon it. He gave him the will for happiness; the happiness he willed; the will for right; free choice, without which he could not have kept to the right which is justice, but which also made it possible for him not to keep to it. Nothing God gave was other than good. Adam exemplified first of all his kind the failure to live as one ought which is not an indication of the powerlessness of free choice, but of its terrible power of destruction (C III.14).

Notes

1   There is perhaps an early example in Gerbert of Aurillac's *De Ratione et Ratione Uti* (PL 139).

2   Aristotle, *De Interpretatione* 18b.

3   Cf. Co 8.

9

Sacraments: the Church and salvation

Anselm held the view, which was not widely or seriously questioned in the controversies of his day, that baptism is necessary for salvation. But he knows that some cannot believe that God condemns unbaptized infants. They say that no one can believe that newly-born children are to be condemned to an eternity of punishment for someone else's sin, that is, for the sin of Adam born in them. Infants have no judgement, and so in any case, they could not be just. If we ourselves forgive our children the faults of their immaturity, surely God ought not to judge them more harshly than we do? Anselm's approach to this classic difficulty about the doctrine of original sin coupled with a strong doctrine of the effect of baptism and its indispensability, which was a particularly strong Augustinian legacy in the West, is to distinguish between the way it is proper for God to act and the way it is proper for men to act.

He applies here exactly the principles we have seen him developing elsewhere, in connection with the notions of divine honour, and of what is properly 'owed' to God by his creatures. A human adult cannot justly reproach a small child for a fault which he himself or she herself shares. God can justly reprove all faults. And there is no question of an obligation in the case of the child and the adult. The infant owes it to his Creator to be what he ought, to be that for which God made him. The adult cannot require that of the child as an absolute obligation to himself, but God can and must. God is just in asking of the infant's nature that which he gave it, and which the infant rightly owes him (Co 28).

But God is also supremely merciful. Ought he not to ignore the infant's failure to be what he or she ought, out of loving-kindness? Here Anselm makes a standard distinction between inborn 'original' sin and the actual sins committed by the individual as a result of original sin. The infant is not guilty of these. So Anselm thinks he ought not to be punished as though he were fully Adam's equal in wrongdoing (Co 22). But again there are considerations of the absolute requirements of the way things ought to be. It seems clear to Anselm the no one can be admitted to heaven who is not perfectly just because that would be a contradiction in terms. He points out that after the Day of Judgement all angels and all human beings must be either in heaven or in hell (Co 23). So it seems to him an inescapable conclusion that even though the sin of unbaptized infants is not as great as that of Adam, they will not be able to enter heaven; and therefore they must be in hell (Co 23).

Anselm says that an inability to do what one ought which derives from a blameworthy act remains inexcusable because of the guilt which remains. In infants God demands from their human nature the righteousness which it received in Adam and Eve, together with the ability to preserve that righteousness which they also received. Their human nature is blameworthy for failing in this, just as was the human nature of Adam and Eve when they fell (C III.7).

Again, this is not merely an abstraction. It has most concrete manifestations. Human nature was visibly diminished by what happened when Adam fell. It became subject to gross and uncontrollable appetites, as Scripture shows. (Here Anselm gives examples.) The Creator was dishonoured by the deformity of his handiwork, just as a human artist would be if his excellent work was shown to the world damaged, so that its imperfections were imputed to him (C III.7).

This is a strong argument for the doctrine of the effect of baptism which Anselm now outlines, distinguishing in the manner fundamental to the rationale of the contemporary penitential system between the guilt and the penalty of sin. In baptism of those to whom the grace of faith is given (and here Anselm seems to couple justification by faith inseparably with the effect of baptism) the inborn defect of righteousness in human nature is forgiven; and at the same time the guilt of being unable to be righteous, and the corruption and damage which dishonours God as Creator. But the actual corruption and the wrong desires are not immediately removed. These are not now, however, in themselves sins as they were before. Only unrighteousness, or injustice, is sin. Otherwise, they would be blotted out in baptism, which removes all traces of sin. And in any case, they are no more than resemblances to the behaviour of the beasts, for the corruption of our nature has simply made us like animals, and we do not call the behaviour proper to animals sinful when it is found in creatures to whom it is natural. The corruption and the wrong desires were sins because they were corrupt in human nature and wrong for human nature, and therefore unjust, not because fleshly appetite is itself a sin. So baptism takes away all the consequences of sin by taking away unrighteousness. But it does not take away the penalty to be paid for sins thereafter committed. That remains, says Anselm, because if the faithful were transformed at once by baptism (or martyrdom, which he includes as purging from all sin), there would be no room for merit; the believer would not be able to exercise the faith and hope which are directed towards things unseen. If everyone could see that to be converted to Christ immediately made one incorruptible, everyone would be converted at once. It is more glorious for us to obtain the happiness of heaven through faith and hope, because in that way we grow by grace and bear fruit (C III.8–9).

Anselm is dealing here with a limited range of concepts and with, as it were, the mechanics of the process. It is characteristic of him that he cannot fudge the issue, and that, although he feels compassion for the plight of the unbaptized baby, he puts the ultimate requirements of what is right and what ought to be so first in the scheme of things, and can come to only one conclusion. He does not enter here into questions touched on in his prayers or explore the complexity of the nature and force of sinfulness in human beings; nor does he speak of the transforming effects of Christ's work within the individual here. He is concerned with a philosophical and theological problem, and he strips it to its essentials. But it is clear from everything we know about him in the conduct of his daily life that he saw with equal clarity both the awfulness of sin not just as an abstraction but in its most intimate workings in the soul, and the supreme importance for eternity of the right relation of all humanity to God.

In the first Christian generations it was usual for baptism to be delayed until near death, or at least given in adult life, on the understanding that it purged the guilt and the penalty of both original sin and all the actual sins the individual had committed, and that it could do so only once. The baptized believer was not expected to fall into sin again. The small daily offences inseparable from human behaviour, a burst of irritation with a friend, a moment's selfishness, could be mended by apology both to the person who had been hurt and to God. One turned back to God, from whom one had momentarily turned away, and asked his forgiveness, and in that way baptism was renewed and not lost. Serious sin was another matter. Apostasy, murder, adultery were taken very seriously by early Christian communities and those who had committed them were excommunicated, as cut off both from the community and from God. One school of thought held that this constituted an irreparable loss of baptism, and since baptism could not be repeated, there was no hope of restoration. Others were prepared to make some machinery available. Normally this consisted in the setting apart of the penitents while they performed acts of penance to demonstrate to the community the sincerity of their repentance, and the insistence that they wear special garments to show that they were postulants for restoration to forgiveness. In due course the local bishop would declare absolution before the whole community, and the penitent would be admitted to communion again, although he would never be quite as he was before (for example, he could not be ordained).

In the late fourth century, during Augustine's lifetime, the seriousness of the peril in which those who died unbaptized stood encouraged parents to bring their children to be baptized as infants, and there was a general shift of practice in the West, so that infant baptism became the norm. This change posed serious theological problems which had not been so clearly apparent before. It brought about a separation between the making of a personal commitment of faith, which now had to be done on the baptized infant's behalf, and the action of baptizing with water in the name of the Trinity. It was this last which was held to be constitutive of baptism, until the concept of personal commitment came to seem of prime importance in the course of the debates of the Reformation. The emphasis in 'believers' baptism' is upon the relationship cemented by baptism between the soul and God. The earlier emphasis had been upon the bringing of the baptized child into the community of the Church and thus upon the role of the Church in the process of salvation. The two are of course not alternatives, but complementary, and many reforming communities retained infant baptism, on the under-standing that the child would be brought up to make his or her own commitment. That is to see baptism not as an event, but as a process in which the ceremony of baptism is decisive. A second entailment of this change to infant baptism was the gradual development of a system of 'private penance'. It was no longer realistic to expect that almost all those who were baptized would keep clear of sin for the rest of their lives. There was need for provision of a less dramatic sort than that provided by the rare and exceptional act of excommunication with restoration by the bishop in public. Among monastic communities, and then to meet a pastoral need among the laity in general, there grew up in and even before Carolingian times, a pattern of making regular confession to a priest. He would enjoin penances according to the seriousness of the sin and declare absolution.

Anselm explores some of the implications of these two developments in his reflections on the effect of baptism in the infant.

If baptism wipes away all sin, it is easy to see that an infant immediately after baptism is sure of heaven. But what of the period of its growing through infancy, before it reaches an age when it can understand the concept of sin and know what it ought to do? During that time it continues to lack uprightness of will and so it seems that it must, if it dies then, fall into hell. On the other hand, if the effect of baptism can be said to operate subsequently to the moment of baptism in these cases, keeping the infant safe until it reaches years of discretion, why cannot baptism act in that way for all, so that there is no need for a penitential system for adults who fall into sin again after baptism (Co 29)? Anselm answers that everything turns on the concept of blameworthiness. Before baptism the inability to be just is culpable. After baptism it is not. So after baptism, in infants, the inability to be just excuses the lack of justice in them. God does not require what is impossible for them (they are too young to will rightly) and what is now not blameworthy in them. So such infants are saved by the justice of Christ, who gave himself for them (Co 29).

Anselm's theology of penance is perfectly in tune with that of the contemporary world, although he gives us glimpses of theoretical under-pinnings which are entirely his own. He was aware of the patristic controversy over the possibility of restoration of the lapsed. He mentions it in connection with the most serious matter of sin among the clergy.

Anselm took particular care over the discipline of corrupt and erring priests (cf. Letter 257), especially those who were refusing to submit to the rule of celibacy which was being applied with unprecedented strictness as a result of recent developments in reform of the church; those who lapsed were another matter. If they show a sufficient evidence of sincerity of repentance and a change of heart, Anselm would like to see them restored. But he knows of patristic texts (Calixtus and Gregory the Great) which suggest that this is by no means a straightforward matter, and he stresses the need to err on the safe side (Letter 65).

As to the power of the keys vested in him, especially as Archbishop, he seems to have taken the view that it is strictly declarative of God's own binding and loosing. 'May all-powerful God absolve you from past sins and keep you without sin in the future', he writes to three errant monks of Bec (Letter 333). 'No man alive can absolve you from these chains of excommunication and these anathemas, unless you do what I lovingly beg and advise you' (Letter 431 to the apostate monk Adrian of Canterbury). But he did not hesitate to use the sanction of excommunication where he thought it a necessary discipline, and to regard it as his duty to do so within the order of things in which he had pastoral charge as archbishop. He threatened excommunication to one secular lord who had been stealing the property of the Church at Canterbury (Letter 358). He confirms an excommunication in characteristic style: 'I, Anselm, archbishop though a sinner, by that authority which God has given me through the archbishopric . . .' (Letter 374).

So Anselm lived at a stage in the development of the penitential system when private confession was well established, and together with it the practice of enjoining penance to be performed in token of sincerity of repentance. He explains in the *Cur Deus Homo* that it is essential to right order that the sinner should make voluntary payment of his debt for the sins he has committed. Otherwise he cannot know the happiness of heaven. Boso had put to him a question which was clearly asked by contemporaries: why, if we thus pay God what we owe him, need we pray 'Forgive us our sins' (CDH I.19)? This supplication is part of the payment, says Anselm. We remain in God's debt whatever we do. It is not fitting for us to speak to him as to an equal, a fellow-man to whom we have paid what we owe and whose forgiveness has thus been made unnecessary (CDH I.19). It is an important aspect of this view of the matter that Anselm sees no incompatibility or disjunction between this human voluntary debt-paying and the one sufficient sacrifice made for man by Christ. When man does all he can, and asks for forgiveness too, he has still not done enough, for he cannot begin to pay what he really owes God. But it is proper for him humbly to try to do what he can. What do you pay to God for your sin? Anselm asks Boso, and Boso replies: 'penitence, a contrite and humble heart, fasting and physical labour of various sorts, acts of mercy in giving and forgiving, obedience'. Then you pay him what is due to him in any case, and would be due to him even if you were not a sinner, answers Anselm (CDH I.20). Man lives in a perpetual relationship of 'owing' to God, because he owes him gratitude and service for his very being. What we call 'penitential tasks' are really not punishments in themselves, though in our sinful condition we may feel them as such; they are the proper actions of a rational creature which loves God in uprightness of will. So in performing them we do not seek to add to the sacrifice of Christ or imply that he has not done enough. We merely do what we ought to do and would have owed to God even if we had not sinned. And because we are unworthy and sinners, we add to that the prayer for forgiveness which Jesus taught us.

It is in this context that we must place Anselm's encouragement to his correspondents to perform good works. In a letter to his nephew Anselm he says, 'Above all guard your acts before men and your heart before God' (Letter 290). In a letter to Burgundius and Richeza he reminds them of the nearness of judgement and tells them to ask themselves constantly, 'How are we satisfying God for our sins?' (Letter 258). This sort of advice is in tune with Anselm's Augustinian view that God has his elect, but they do not know who they are. Never take your election for granted, he exhorts several of his friends. Few are chosen, and we cannot know how few they are (Letter 51; cf. 167, 184).

He was always inclined to compassion towards those who fell away and returned repentant. He begs Adrian, apostate monk of Canterbury, to return (Letter 431). He asks Abbot Lambert to receive back his lost sheep (Letter 197). Monks who had fled their houses were the most common instance we hear of in the letters (cf. Letters 105, 140, 141, 143), but we may safely infer that Anselm approached the hearing of confession in the same spirit of mercy with everyone.

Clergy who are resisting the legislation about celibacy are continuing to hear confessions and give absolution and bury the dead, Anselm hears. All these tasks may be carried out by senior monks (*monachis provectioris aetatis*). Anyone may baptize, for it is Christ who baptizes (*quicumque baptizet, Christus baptizat*). There is therefore no reason why the people should suffer in the interim before worthy substitutes can be appointed if these clergy are cast out of their benefices. Anselm calls on the laity, great and lowly, to co-operate in expelling such priests (Letter 254).

This is a letter of some importance for Anselm's theology of ministry. It tells us that the Eucharist was not of prime importance as a regular event in parish life, but that the forgiveness of sins was central; and it allows a role to those who are not priests in the sacrament of penance which would have been denied them later.

Theological debate over the Eucharist did not yet touch on the questions of sacrifice and the related matter of the priestliness of the ordained ministry which preoccupied thinkers of the Reformation period. The doctrine of transubstantiation was another matter. Anselm's master Lanfranc had become embroiled in a debate with the grammarian Berengar, and it was out of this that the doctrine of transubstantiation had first clearly been formulated. Berengar had argued that it was against common sense and the laws of nature to say that bread and wine actually become the body and blood of Christ. The Church had responded by trying to define in precisely what manner they do so, and leaving a legacy of concern with the manner not the fact of the change to later generations. [1] Anselm kept out of this debate, although it was still alive in his generation; Gilbert Crispin his pupil and friend and later abbot of Westminster wrote a treatise on the subject.

We may take it that Anselm took Lanfranc's view and that this reason for not making a contribution was that dislike of controversy which is so consistent in him throughout his lifetime. It is true, too, perhaps, here as elsewhere in his remarks on questions concerning the sacraments, that he himself had no sense of either pastoral or intellectual dissatisfaction with the way things were done and the way they were understood in his day.

Anselm's most substantial writing on the Eucharist was occasioned by controversy between Greek and Latin Christians. Among the doctrinal differences which had helped to precipitate the split of 1054 between East and West had been a disagreement as to whether leavened or unleavened bread should be used in the Eucharist. Shortly before his death Anselm sent Walram, bishop of Naumburg, a copy of his treatise on the Procession of the Holy Spirit and wrote him a letter. In it, he considers the Scriptural evidence about the question of leavened or unleavened bread. We know that at the Last Supper, because it was the Passover meal, unleavened bread would have been used, but nowhere does Christ specify in anything he said that leavened or unleavened bread is to be used. Both are bread, says Anselm, and they differ in substance no more than the old man full of the 'leaven' of sin is different in substance from the new man who is freed from his sins. The Old Testament emphasis upon unleavened bread was necessary as a sign and as an admonishment. But we have now passed from that foreshadowing to the reality, says Anselm; we eat the 'unleavened' flesh of Christ. And so we do not need this old symbolism in the bread which is consecrated so as to become this flesh (S I.1). This is the essence of the matter.

Nevertheless, it is clearly better to consecrate unleavened bread because that is what the Lord did and that is what is more appropriate. If the Greeks say that in so doing the Western Christians are adopting a Jewish practice and continuing to observe the Old Law, that would be to impute the same fault to Christ (S I.2–3).

The Greeks may reply that there is still a symbolic meaning in the use of unleavened bread. However the symbolism is understood, says Anselm, there can be no intention in the Latin practice of implying anything other than that Jesus came without sin. Surely the Greeks do not want to say that there is no place for symbols in the Christian life? Baptism is acknowledged to be the symbol of someone's death and burial. Or if they want to exclude just those symbols used by the Jews, they should avoid baptizing with water. One by one Anselm takes the Scriptural passages which the Greeks are quoting and explains their meaning.

Walram was greatly distressed by what he learned of differences in custom among the Churches. For, he wrote to Anselm, 'God is undivided Trinity, and those who are in God are one in him. Diversity in the Church is directly opposed to unity. And what is divided against itself cannot stand.' Palestinian Christians believe one thing about the sacraments, Armenians another, Rome and Gaul still differently. The practices used in celebrating the Eucharist differ. He points, over and above the question of the use of unleavened bread, to diversity in the consecration. The practice with which he is familiar, and which he believes to derive directly from Christ and to be supported by long usage, is to bless the bread and the chalice separately, making the sign of the Cross over each. He wonders how different practices can have arisen. He raises the question of covering the chalice with a cloth from the outset, to signify the shroud which was found in the sepulchre. That seems to him a wrong practice, for Christ was crucified naked and there should be no veil over his sacrifice. He has no objection to the Western practice of covering the consecrated elements at the end, so as to protect them and keep them clean.

Anselm answered his letter by agreeing that it would indeed be a good and praiseworthy thing if practices were the same everywhere. But he himself takes the view that what matters is agreement about the fundamental importance of the Eucharist, its efficacy. His own position is that it is better to preserve harmony by tolerating such differences of practice as do not touch this central concern. Walram asks how differences can have arisen. Anselm thinks it is no more than a reflection of the infinite variability of human nature. He explores for Walram the implications of the two differences of practice he has mentioned, and shows him that it can be argued both that a single sign of the Cross is proper and that two are right; and that the chalice should be covered from the beginning and that it should not (S III.1–3).

It is clear, then, that Anselm saw the Church as playing a clear, necessary and well defined role in the process of salvation for the individual and for the world, and especially so through her ministry of the sacraments. Once more it is a question of order and harmony, of understanding what is important and integral to the patterns of the Church's life and worship. He was not disturbed by differences which do not grate on these.

Note

1   cf. ARCIC, *Agreed Statement on the Eucharist* (Windsor, 1971) 6, note 2, and see the forthcoming papers of the 1988 Conference on Berengar at Wolfenbüttel.

Conclusion

Although it is perfectly clear that Anselm stands within a Western and especially Augustinian tradition and proceeds accordingly on certain assumptions, there is no mistaking his originality. He took the Latin Aristotle and the Augustinian Platonism and the Roman grammar and rhetoric in which his mind was trained, and the ideas about social order which governed contemporary feudal society, and did some fresh thinking with them. The ideas of 'order' and 'doing what one ought' gave him a fierce intellectual pleasure. He found by applying them that he could unravel many of the classic knots of Western Christian theology. The 'most famous question' of the relationship of God's will to the will of man, the question why it was necessary for God to redeem mankind as he did, the problem of evil, all fell away into clarity and simplicity before these principles. No one had attempted anything of the kind before him. He was the first to notice certain characteristics of the behaviour of the Latin language in use: the ways in which a particular grammatical form is sometimes used with a quite different application from what appears on the surface in the case of words such as 'can' and 'must', and even 'do'. He was the first to attempt to show how the reality of God's existence is bound up with the very nature of human understanding.

There are limitations in this sort of approach. It is—although also deeply spiritual—essentially highly cerebral. It makes use of human experience at the level of understanding, that is, of our experiences of knowing things, and observing nature, but not of emotional experience. Anselm's expression of feeling in the *Proslogion* and in the prayers and meditations is impassioned but stylized. There is nothing of the muddle and approximation of the bulk of human experience. There is an understanding of the deep structures of language and of its effective power, but not of its capacity for nuance and its capriciousness. The God to whom the *Proslogion* argument reaches out would have been intelligible outside the Christian tradition to anyone familiar with Platonic thinking. These limitations are the obverse of Anselm's strengths as a thinker, and they do not diminish his achievement. But they do encourage us to look critically at his influence and at the value his work has for our own day.

Anselm's immediate influence was considerable. He made many friends during his lifetime, and his writings had a wide circulation, finding their way into monastic libraries all over Europe. He became, within a generation of his death, one of the few latter-day authors to be commonly included in *florilegia* of quotations from the Fathers (Hugh of St Victor and Bernard of Clairvaux were his usual companions from among the moderns). In the academic community of the twelfth century, where energies were bent on the construction of syllabuses and the development of a university system, he was not greatly favoured, because his books did not lend themselves to the sort of brisk coverage required, and because his technical skills began to seem a little dated as the study of logic and language progressed and technical terminology and principles became more sophisticated. But the solid theological worth of his thought brought him back into favour by the beginning of the thirteenth century, when the Friars in particular made use of him. His devotional writings held a huge readership and attracted many imitators throughout the Middle Ages.

On the topics of sixteenth-century debate which divided Western Christendom—justification, faith and works, the relation of Scripture and tradition, authority in the Church—we have seen that Anselm has a good deal to say. Certain points seemed to him not at all controversial. Faith is nothing, he says, unless it is made alive by love (M 78). Justification seemed to him to involve a real and full restoration not a mere imputing of justice (CDH I.19). He understood justice as definable in terms of truth and rightness and being as one ought (V 12). He thought good works important as a demonstration of sincerity of repentance, and, like other monastic theologians of the eleventh and twelfth centuries, he exhorted Christians to take seriously the need to live a holy life if they were to be admitted to the heavenly City, never taking their election for granted, but holding their faith in holy dread of judgement. He expected Scripture and tradition to harmonize; although Scripture is always primary for him, and his theology is systematically Biblically based, he applied reason to its interpretation and looked to the Church's teaching as corroboration. He understood very well that ministry is service, and the highest powers of the keys exercised by those who are themselves sinners and in need of forgiveness, but he did not see that as incompatible with discipline.

All this was in a context where ecclesiology had not yet been subjected to the strains of later mediaeval developments and he had no reason to see any possibility of disjunction between personal and communal Christian life, the direct action of grace in the individual and the Church's ministry of Word and sacrament. But that does not mean that his solutions to the problems he did perceive are of no relevance to the sixteenth-century debates or to modern ecumenical attempts to resolve them. At a number of points he got behind the issues as they were later to be presented and provided matter of continuing usefulness. Perhaps the most significant of his achievements here is the account he gives of the action of grace and his emphasis upon justification as constituting a real and full restoration of the sinner worked out in the course of a lifetime of growth in holiness. To the debates with Orthodox Christians, already going on in his lifetime, he made his contribution in the treatise on the Procession of the Holy Spirit and the letters on the sacraments.

In reading Anselm we are in the presence not only of a man of quite exceptional holiness and deep spirituality, but also of one of the best minds of the Western world. He stood far above his contemporaries in the subtlety and clarity of his thinking and in his capacity to see new solutions to old difficulties.

When Anselm's *Cur Deus Homo* was finished he sent it to Pope Urban II with a letter of justification for such theological endeavours. He speaks of the way in which those whose hearts are purified of sin by faith take delight in contemplating the reasonableness of what they believe. The early Fathers wrote about the faith not only so as to confound heresies, but also for this higher reason. Perhaps we cannot hope in later days to equal their achievements, but they did not say all that could be said in their short lives. This reasonableness of truths of faith is so deep and large that it cannot be exhausted by mortal effort. There is always more to say, and the Lord continues to impart his gifts of grace to the Church. So the theologian has God's work to do. And that delight in understanding which is so apparent in Anselm himself brings the Christian closer to the sight of God himself which is the end and purpose of his life.